How to Grow

Winter Vegetables

How to Grow Winter Vegetables

CHARLES DOWDING

First published in 2011 by

Green Books,
Foxhole, Dartington,
Totnes, Devon TQ9 6EB

Photographs by Charles Dowding except for the following:
Jack Dowding: page 8. Susie Dowding: page 71.
Steph Hafferty: pages 39, 59, 70, 144, 159 (top), 164, 166, 194, 224.
Lucy Pope: pages 44, 75, 100, 115, 160 (left), 161-2, 165 (bottom), 167 (bottom), 174, 175 (top three), 176, 179, 184 (left), 196, 206.

Design by Jayne Jones
Cover design by Stephen Prior / Jayne Jones

ISBN 978 1 900322 88 1

Printed on Revive 75 White Silk 75% recycled paper
by Latimer Trend, Plymouth, UK

Cover image: 'Lusia' chicory, November.
Back cover images: Left: 'Sanguina' beetroot, October. Middle: 'Ibis' celeriac, October. Right: 'Apex F1' Chinese cabbage, late November.
Page 2: 'Sai Sai' leaf radish, November. Pages 10-11: 'Redbor F1' kale, December. Pages 28-9: 'Early Purple Sprouting' broccoli, late November. Pages 78-9: 'Barbosa' savoy cabbage, December. Pages 146-7: 'Tardiva' chicory hearting up in November. Pages 170-1: Softneck garlic hung to dry in a barn. Pages 186-7: Salad in December.

Contents

Acknowledgements

Thanks to my family and especially Susie for their support. Edward's eyes were raised to the skies when I accepted the commission, and he remarked "We know where you'll be this winter." Thanks also to Amanda Cuthbert for the idea (after finding her plot annoyingly empty last winter), to Alethea Doran for incredibly thorough editing, and to all the team at Green Books.

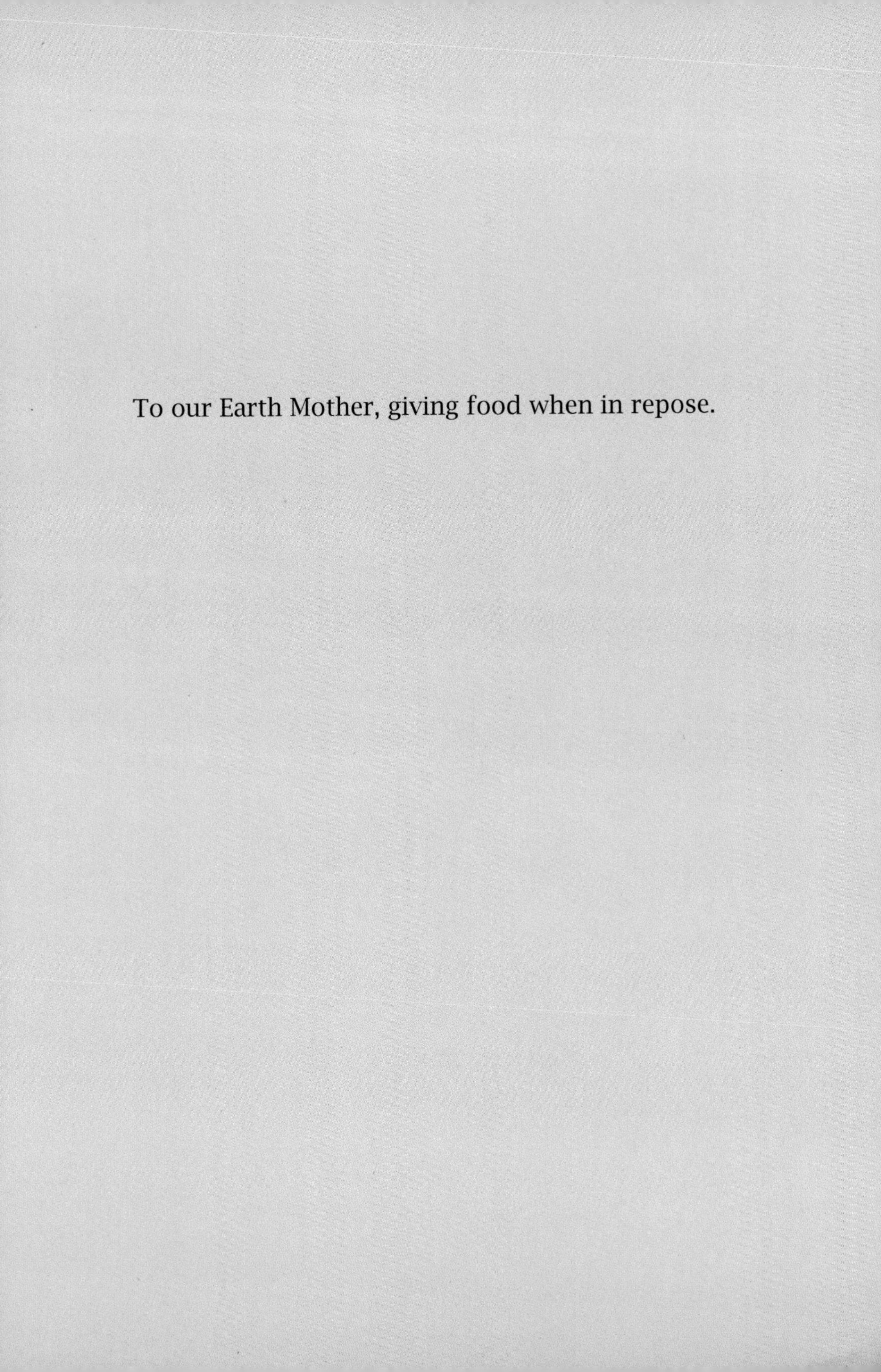

To our Earth Mother, giving food when in repose.

Introduction

Welcome to the amazingly varied world of winter produce. This book sets out to widen your winter horizons, revealing the many vegetables that can be grown and enjoyed in the year's darker half. Fresh vegetables in winter are even more welcome than in summer – some green to alleviate the grey, and flavours that have been sweetened by frost.

You can also enjoy stored harvests, for example, vegetables from sacks in the shed, or ropes of onion and garlic that have been stored under cover.

Some of these vegetables take the main part of a year to grow and mature. Others can be sown after midsummer – even in September for winter salad – to grow indoors.

I also aim to help you plan and practise a yearly cycle of gardening, so that the harvests of your vegetables in the winter can match the harvests made in summer from the same ground. It is possible to keep sowing and planting through summer so that something is always growing and there is less 'feast or famine'. Many vegetables for winter eating can be slotted into a plot that is also producing regular meals in summer.

Part 2 includes several chapters of background advice to do with soil and compost, the foundation of good gardening. Harvests are immeasurably better when plants are growing healthily in fertile soil. In Part 3 I offer the essential knowledge required to grow each vegetable, especially the best time to sow – vital information that is often overlooked.

Sowing at the right time helps reduce losses from pests and diseases. The advice here should enable you to unleash the powerful combination of soil's ability to confer health to plants, and seeds' ability to launch into healthy growth once they have germinated at the most propitious moment.

Parts 4 and 5 give advice on when and how to harvest your vegetables, either for immediate use or for storage – because harvesting and storing is as important as growing.

I hope you will glean many tips here that are relevant to your soil (or growing medium) and the amount of time available to you, enabling you to grow healthy plants and harvest them at the best moment. Then you can enter winter with the warming knowledge that a tasty harvest is growing or is safely stored.

Left: Spreading cow manure in December after a harvest of chicory hearts.

PART 1

Winter's Potential

Chapter 1

A forgotten season

Making the most of winter's amazing possibilities

Winter can offer vegetables in two ways: fresh harvests, such as leeks and salad leaves, and produce such as carrots and onions that have been stored from earlier harvests in the summer and autumn. Having these vegetables to hand can make a huge difference to one's health and well-being through the seemingly long months of cold and dark. The secret to having this produce in winter is to grow throughout the year and to start sowing as early as possible in the spring.

Winter's two parts

What do I mean by winter? A precise definition by time is difficult when the seasons overlap so much, and changes in the weather can sometimes make it feel like winter in October and also in April. This book covers the winter half-year, as opposed to the summer half-year, and I define it in two parts.

True winter is under way by December, when growth is almost halted, and continues until March or even April, by which time daylight and some early warmth have returned, although there are still very few fresh vegetables to eat.

Then, in April, May and even into June in a cold spring, there can be a long and frustrating wait for plants to grow and mature. Although the weather may be fine and warm, there is surprisingly little to eat from the garden, in a period known as the 'hungry gap' – a kind of 'second winter' in food terms. In the past this period was occasionally characterised by famine as people waited for the first new harvests, such as broad beans.

This book will help you grow vegetables for true winter as well as for this hungry period, winter's shadow. You need to garden many months ahead, with sowings of purple sprouting broccoli in June, spring cabbages in August, broad beans in October or November and spinach in early March, all for harvests in the hungry gap.

You will also find lots of advice on helping vegetables survive winter in better shape and then grow strongly again in the spring. A cover

Right: 'Cavolo Nero' kale in early December.

Swede, lamb's lettuce and purple sprouting broccoli – for harvesting over a long period.

of netting, barely visible, can be enough to lessen the effects of frost, wind and snow so that plants endure when they would otherwise have perished. Using fleece in the spring brings growth forwards dramatically. Both of these are simple to use and cheap to buy.

Summer & winter vegetables contrasted

Growing vegetables in summer is a busier activity than in winter, partly because winter vegetables need to be sown, planted and weeded in summer. If the summer is wet and the tomatoes are poor, at least your winter vegetables will be growing well.

Periods of harvest

An important difference between summer and winter vegetables is that in summer many plants – such as courgettes, runner beans and tomatoes – offer repeated harvests over a long period. Continual summer warmth encourages harvests from the same plants for some time. This can result in summer gluts, and perhaps even some complacency, because winter harvests do not repeat, or do so only slowly.

In fact, most winter vegetables, such as cabbage hearts, leeks and parsnips, offer one harvest only. There is little new growth in winter, so it needs to have happened in spring, summer and autumn. During all this preparation time – as long as six to eight months – the gardener is busy but unrewarded until the season of harvest finally arrives.

Fortunately there are also some fast-growing winter vegetables to sow in summer, such as salads, kale and turnips, which fill the gaps left after summer harvests. The sowing calendar in Part 3 has as much to say about July to October as it does about March to June.

Summer weather for winter harvests

Summer weather plays an important part in growing for winter, and it helps to be aware of a marked difference in the weather needed for different plants. For instance, most *summer* vegetables grow fast, offer their harvests in fine weather and do best in seasons of plentiful warmth, without too many long periods of rain and damp.

However, in Britain at least, the weather does not always behave like that, so tomatoes can be blighted, beans may rot and sweetcorn

After a wet August, leeks and kale of many varieties are flourishing. Under the fleece is Chinese cabbage.

may not ripen before winter arrives. These are all immensely discouraging experiences.

But all is not lost: at the same time, summers of cool, damp weather are excellent for many *winter* vegetables.

We cannot predict weather in advance but, by growing a range of vegetables that have different likes and dislikes, the chances of success are generally increased. A damp Atlantic climate is actually as good for many winter vegetables as it is tricky for many summer ones, so if you live in such an area this book has much to offer!

Take advantage of cool, wet summers & autumns

* Brussels sprouts, leeks and parsnips thrive in wet summers – indeed, they are often healthier in these conditions, with less rust on leeks and fewer caterpillars eating the sprout plants.

- Wet Augusts are superb for sowing and growing many winter salads.
- Damp, soggy autumns help plants to carry on growing by lessening early frost.

A mild late January. From left: broad beans emerging, leaf beet, purple sprouting broccoli and garlic.

Garden ahead for winter

The best harvests for winter are achieved by good soil preparation and sowing the first seeds as soon as winter ends.

Best sowing dates

Many vegetables grow quite slowly, and some sowings for winter, such as celeriac and parsnip, need to be made as early as March. Every month has a 'best time' for sowing at least one winter vegetable, so it is not a matter of popping all your seeds in at once. Kale and savoy cabbage can be sown as late as June; indeed they often grow more healthily if sown slightly later than is recommended on the seed packet.

July and August are busy times for sowing winter salads, so I recommend that you make a note in your calendar of the timings given in Part 3, in order to be prepared with seeds when they will have the best chance of growing you a good harvest.

Making soil fertile

The other aspect of being prepared for winter is the condition of the soil in your plot – how healthy and fertile it is. Good soil grows great vegetables, and I give advice on how to achieve this, mainly in Chapters 3 and 4. My speciality is growing without digging, and there are lots of tips here for managing this, but if you enjoy digging you can skip over the no-dig parts of Chapter 3 and concentrate on the rest of the book.

I also garden without using any packet fertiliser or synthetic sprays, and have evolved methods of treating soil and growing vegetables that have more chance of working in an organic garden or allotment. In order to avoid dealing with unexpected problems and coping with disappointing losses, I suggest that you familiarise yourself with the potential pitfalls of pests and diseases, then garden in a way to minimise the risk of encountering them. That is the philosophy behind all my advice, and I trust it will help your growing to be successful, with less need for artificial inputs.

Stored food

In addition to delicious fresh harvests from the garden, a great deal of winter food can be stored, either in the house or in a cool, dry place outdoors.

An indoor larder

When your winter vegetables have grown to maturity there will be a long period of harvest. This is divided into two parts. In the first you are harvesting vegetables to store – starting as early as July, with garlic maturing. In the second part you are harvesting fresh from the garden, throughout winter. Two things stand out here.

- The first is to harvest each vegetable at its best time so that it comes out of the soil in a healthy state. For example, garlic will sprout if left in the ground too long and then won't keep so well, while potatoes may be infected by blight or eaten by slugs. See the monthly calendar in Chapter 10 for advice on the harvest requirements of each vegetable.
- The second is how best to store each harvest made during summer and autumn, and even sometimes in winter. Each vegetable has slightly different requirements for keeping: some keep better in the warmth of a house; some in cool but frost-free darkness; others in a cold outdoor environment, just sheltered from the rain. All this is explained in Part 5.

An outdoor larder

There is one thing that no stored vegetables can offer: fresh, green leaves, always welcome at a time when any fresh food is so scarce.

Swedes, leeks and chicory still to harvest at the turn of the year. Dig/no-dig experiment in the beds behind.

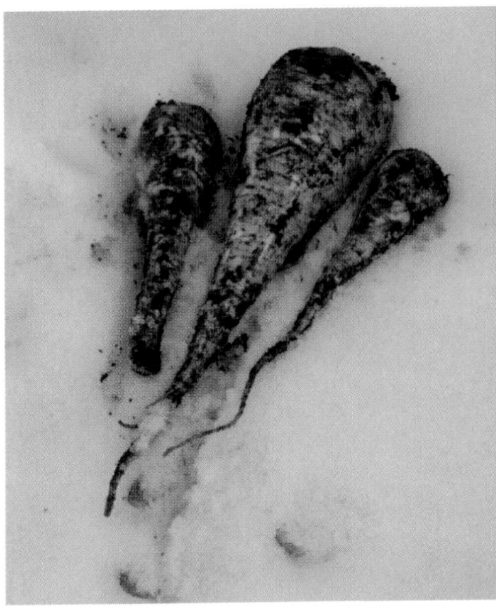

Storing *in situ*

Some root vegetables, especially swedes and parsnips, store well in the soil. They are high-value food – indeed parsnips were a main winter staple before the arrival of potatoes. Once germinated (the tricky part) parsnips are relatively easy to grow, extremely easy to store for the winter, in the soil they grew in, and their flavour improves with each cold snap as starches turn to sugar. Other winter vegetables do not benefit so much from cold weather but still survive it.

These 'White Gem' parsnips were dug after a week of severe frost. Snow had kept the soil soft.

Success at harvesting leaves such as kale and salad, as well as green vegetables such as Brussels sprouts, depends on three things:

- the weather, which we cannot control
- our choice of suitable varieties, and growing them well enough that they have more ability to withstand severe weather
- any protection we can give them.

When this goes well, the plot or garden can serve as a food store for gathering leaves off the same plants, over a long period. See Chapter 11 for tips on better ways of picking so that plants are able to continue producing for longer, often into spring.

Sow at the best moment

* The key to success for all winter salads is sowing them at the right moment in late summer – early enough that they have grown to a good size before winter begins, but also late enough that they have not started to mature before winter sets in.

Some salads are winter hardy to a certain point only. See Chapter 14, pages 192-3, for how to protect them with cloches, and Chapter 15 for growing them in a greenhouse or polytunnel, where they will withstand being frozen at night and can then grow a little in the relative warmth of any sunlit winter and spring days.

'D'Orlanda' lamb's lettuce in January, having just survived a week of frosts down to -9°C (16°F).

Being outside in winter

Growing winter vegetables has another advantage, besides all the good things it gives us to eat. It takes us outdoors, sometimes in nasty weather and also on days of lovely low sunlight. However chilled we may feel, the experience is always invigorating – often warming in a way – and winter can be a quietly uplifting time, especially on days when there are hints of spring just around the corner.

A particular benefit of spending time outside in winter is the extra daylight one can absorb. When inside I notice how days can seem utterly miserable, dark and gloomy, yet on going out it feels much lighter and less depressing, quickly lifting my mood.

The vegetable plot also benefits from our attention throughout winter, even though there are far fewer jobs than in summer. Weeds have not entirely stopped growing, and it is really worthwhile to do a little winter weeding, keeping the soil clean in readiness for early spring sowings. Then, as soon as harvests are finished, ground can be cleared and vegetable residues composted, so that by winter's end the whole plot is either growing something or is pristinely prepared for spring.

Winter's first snowfall, with leaves still on apple trees in my orchard.

Chapter 2

A winter's scene

Tips for understanding and adapting to winter

The dark background

Certain aspects of winter are different every year, most noticeably the temperature. Perhaps because of the dramatic alternations between mild and cold winters, we overlook a feature of winter that is equally important to gardening and that never varies: light.

A lack of light

Daylight in winter is in short supply and limits new growth even on days of mild sunshine. In my work I observe the growth of salad plants through autumn, winter and spring, and they have taught me fascinating things about the effects of day length on growth. Plants in the greenhouse and polytunnels are most revealing because although they often have sufficient warmth to grow, they are, even in milder weather, clearly restricted by the short days.

Midwinter lulls

The lowest point in terms of new growth depends on your location. Here in Somerset there is almost a hibernation of plants from mid-December to mid-February, especially when temperatures are low. Any new growth at this time is often from plants converting stored energy into leaves, as with the appearance of snowdrops in February, growing from the energy in their bulbs.

There is a month or so on either side of this period when growth is possible, but it depends a lot on the temperature. This is most apparent with newly planted seeds – for instance, broad beans, which can be sown in late October to early November. Even in a mild autumn they grow very slowly, while an early onset of cold can keep them almost invisible.

Yet even in midwinter, plants can grow new roots, with more of winter's growth happening underground than above. This means that when milder conditions occur in late winter, new leaves can more rapidly be created by the existing roots. Overwintered broad beans and garlic can grow at surprising speeds in March, using the energy of their winter-grown root network, at a time when newly sown seeds barely grow at all.

Right: Salads under cloche and fleece are protected from the snow.

How winter changes growth

- **Smaller leaves is the most striking difference.** Through October especially, my salad plants seem to shrink, even though, particularly in mild weather, they are growing lots of new leaves. Every autumn I find it bizarre that this can happen, but thankfully the reverse process occurs between February and March, when the same plants suddenly increase in size again. As well as the plants growing more leaves, each leaf is larger and heavier.
- **Diminution of quality.** Through autumn, leaves become thinner and duller, and are more likely to be damaged by slugs and to suffer fungal problems. Pests and diseases affect weak specimens, so this tells us how winter is weakening plants, even though they may be able to survive and still grow a little.
- **Colour changes.** Some of the alterations in leaf growth and quality are also due to temperature. Ruby chard goes from being bright green with red veins to a duller and dark red colour all over, for about three months, before reverting to a lusty green in late winter. 'Grenoble Red' lettuce becomes beautifully bronzed, even crimson at times in January and February, then grows greener by March.

This is why there is a 'hungry gap' in spring, when plants are still growing, fast, but are often not mature until early summer. On the other hand, overwintered plants have picked up from where they left off in the autumn, with all their established leaves and roots to propel new growth in early spring.

The first shoots of broad beans, sown in November, emerging through winter snow.

All these observations lead us back to the importance of sowing in good time and at the right time, if we want good vegetables to eat in winter and spring.

Vegetables for winter

So what might a winter garden contain in the way of vegetables for harvesting between about December and April? Here I offer some ideas to help you imagine what is worth growing, in four categories according to how much space and protection each vegetable needs.

The first four vegetables and some of the salad plants too belong to the same plant genus called Brassicaceae, the cabbage family. Their attributes that interest us most in winter are the ability to resist frost and continual wetness, and being able to make new leaves in weather that keeps most vegetables dormant.

Remember that successful winter harvests depend on the soil being in good condition,

A delicacy in late winter

Purple sprouting broccoli is a vigorous plant which, as with many brassicas, can make new leaves and shoots at relatively low temperatures. As long as plants have had enough time to grow to a good size, and have survived any extreme frosts and grazing by pigeons, they can use their established roots and leaves to make delicious new shoots of broccoli in any mild winter weather. Timing of broccoli growth depends on variety.

This 'Early Purple Sprouting' is already making broccoli in November. These heads withstood frosts of -6°C (21°F).

with sufficient organic matter and good drainage. I have found that this is best achieved by surface composting without any digging or cultivation – see Chapter 3, pages 32-8, for advice on soil.

Large spaces

- **Brussels sprouts,** when given plenty of room and also a long period of growth, offer tasty harvests in winter, when cold weather helps to sweeten their flavour.

Four varieties of kale in January – 'Sutherland', 'Red Russian', 'Redbor F1' and 'Pentland Brig'.

- **Kale** is probably the easiest green leaf to grow for winter harvest and is one of the hardiest. There is a good choice of varieties with a range of colours and leaf shapes, and there are also flat-leaved kales, which taste sweet in salad.
- **Purple sprouting broccoli** is mostly for early spring, but some varieties, such as 'Rudolph', can make new shoots in milder midwinter weather.

Medium spaces

- **Cabbage** can cover a long season according to the variety you grow – do make sure you buy seed or plants of varieties that heart up (more or less) at the time you hope to be eating them – for instance, 'January King' (although this one may mature any time between November and February). Savoy cabbages are the hardiest of all, and late varieties of savoy will heart up from February to early April at a time when greens are extremely precious.

Swedes survive frost and snow. This one is 'Helenor', sown in early June.

Small spaces

Some salad plants, although making little new growth in winter, are able to resist most frost and keep their leaves in reasonable health outdoors. Corn salad (lamb's lettuce) is the most reliable and maintains a lusty green colour at all times. Land cress is equally hardy but suffers more from slugs and birds. Winter purslane resists frost and pests but sometimes discolours in midwinter.

Winter harvests under cover

If some protection can be afforded, especially for salad plants, the possibilities for new growth are multiplied many times. In the severe weather of early 2010 I had a cloche full of lettuce, rocket, mustard, endive and chicory, which endured temperatures of -15°C (5°F) and long spells of dull, wet weather. By March they were nearly all growing strongly again.

- **Swede** grows little in winter but is extremely frost hardy and can safely be left in the soil for harvesting when needed. Sometimes my swedes have all their leaves eaten by pigeons yet still sit proudly and in good condition until early April. Swede has a more solid and sweet flesh than its cousin the turnip, which is less frost hardy and best stored indoors.
- **Parsnip** is the king of winter roots, much denser, sweeter, hardier and stronger tasting than potatoes. Parsnips sit happily in the soil all winter, ready for harvesting when needed at any point until about late April, when new growth takes goodness out of their roots.
- **Leeks** are not all capable of surviving hard frost, so be sure to choose a variety such as 'Bandit' or 'Atlanta' if you want harvests in a cold winter. Leeks can put on a lot of new growth in March and up to the end of April, so are a most welcome addition to the small group of hungry gap vegetables.

This winter purslane is frozen but recovered well: winter salads have a great ability to survive large amounts of frost.

Larger structures offer even more possibilities: Part 6 explains how to grow a regular supply of winter salad leaves under cover.

The plot in winter

Winter harvests can get right in the way of digging. Here is another reason for swapping the digging fork or spade for a manure fork. 'No dig' means literally that, and works best when some well-rotted compost or manure is spread on top of the soil. This can even be done when vegetables are still in the ground, giving more time for frost and weather to break up lumps in surface compost.

Keeping organic matter on top of the soil, instead of digging it in, is good for soil health and will lead to excellent vegetables the next year and onwards. Aim to use materials that are

'Bandit' leeks, which grew large in April after surviving long periods of frost and snow.

dark and well broken down, rather than fibrous mulches, which encourage too many slugs.

Not disturbing soil also results in less weed growth, although you will still need to remove the occasional ones. During winter, weeding should continue in mild weather: clean soil means that as soon as the remains of winter vegetables are cleared after harvesting, the soil is ready for sowing and planting in the spring.

See the next chapter for more about the no-dig approach.

Protecting your food

Some winter harvests will be noticed and perhaps eaten by birds and animals unless they are protected in some way.

Netting

Animals can be hungrier than us in winter, birds above all. Pigeons adore brassicas and netting is often necessary. Although a net can be simply draped over the plants, this often does not suffice because birds can sit on top and peck at leaves through holes in the mesh. A structure of stakes is needed, such as 1.5m (5') wooden sticks with a small upside-down flowerpot on top of each one, to support the netting at a height well above the plants.

However, covering crops with netting like this is time consuming and makes harvesting awkward. Also, in spells of heavy snowfall the netting can be pulled down and even broken by the weight of snow. But there is an interesting advantage to netting which compensates somewhat. I discovered it after a

This netting was subsequently weighed down by snow, but the kale survived pecking by pigeons.

A plastic cloche over lamb's lettuce in December snow. After the snow melted, there was little difference between these plants and some next door that had been covered in snow, but by February the cloched plants were larger.

spell of frosts down to about -15°C (5°F), when two-thirds of my purple sprouting broccoli was killed by the cold. Two miles away, on similar soil and in similar conditions, plants from the same sowing survived, and the only difference was a cover of black plastic netting. I think that this gave just enough protection from wind and cold to enable the netted plants to survive.

I use heavy-duty 'anti-bird' net with a mesh size of 2.5cm (1") and a life expectancy of ten years. A 4m (13') roll works well for covering 1.2m (4') beds, because the net can be stretched longer or wider accordingly.

Cloches & fleece

A winter cloche offers a little extra protection, although it does not keep all frost out and plants are frozen for almost as long as those outside, especially in midwinter when sunlight is so weak and limited.

Yet, despite the cold, the cloche is protecting plants from most of the wind, and also from the dampness caused by rain and snow, which evaporates so little in winter. Drier leaves, particularly of salads, survive the cold in better condition, and also suffer less slug damage.

This is also why fleece is less useful in winter than in spring, unless it is suspended above plants on hoops of wire. A fleece cloche works best in reasonably sheltered spots because it is more fragile than plastic and is liable to being torn by winter gales. Then from late February, as the sun starts to dry soil and leaves, fleece can be laid directly on top of plants, small seedlings especially, to protect them from both animals and cold winds. See Part 6 for detailed advice on cloches and fleece.

Keeping wild animals at bay

Growing under cover has an extra advantage beyond protection from the weather: plastic, glass and fleece also serve to keep plants safe from wild animals. For instance, one September my winter salads were being nibbled quite hard by a rabbit or hare, until I erected a cloche over them in early October. The cloche sides did not always touch the soil, so the rabbit could have slipped underneath and into a bed of lovely salad plants, but it never did, and I find that most animals, badgers excepted, are quite nervous of plastic.

PART 2

Preparing for winter

Chapter 3

Looking after your soil

Ways of improving fertility and reducing weeds

Care of the soil is fundamental to growing an abundance of healthy plants. You may sow the best seeds at the best time and care for them in the best way, but that effort will be poorly repaid if the soil has not been well looked after.

For many gardeners this involves digging over the plot, to a depth that suits the gardener's fitness and desire to supposedly 'help the vegetables to send down their roots'. Many people enjoy digging as a vigorous winter activity, but if you don't, the good news is that excellent vegetables can be grown without doing it.

The main part of this chapter is about improving soil in a no-dig way, based on my long experience and also on the successful growing I see in many other gardens and allotments that have not been dug.

The no-dig approach

Avoiding an annual dig involves learning a few new skills, especially with regard to weeds.

Why dig?

When people ask me why I do not dig, I start off by putting the question the other way round: why dig? Digging is so universally seen as a basic necessity – summed up by this message I received:

"I just looked up No Dig – that looks interesting. I think I need to know how to dig first before not doing so, rather along the lines of learning to paint first before going abstract!"

When I ask gardeners why they dig or rotovate, they generally reply that their soil is too hard, so digging opens it up to let the air in. Also they want the loose soil on top to be weathered into a fine tilth for sowing. A third reason is to incorporate manure and organic matter into the rooting zone, where it is thought to be most useful, and digging offers the chance to bury any unwanted weeds or green sward, as well as pulling out roots of perennials such as docks and bindweed.

Looking at each of these reasons in turn, from the point of view of not digging, I hope you

Right: Onion plants in late May. This bed of rich, black soil was mulched with cow manure six months earlier.

will see that they can all be addressed without any cultivation, and that not digging benefits the soil in other ways that digging cannot.

Hard soil?

I know this feeling all too well, because ten years ago I took on a quarter acre of heavy clay soil that had been significantly compacted by large tractors. It is the wettest corner at the bottom of a slope in a field where, after ploughing, there is always a struggle to create a fine enough tilth for sowing.

This soil was full of unpleasant-smelling grey and orange lumps of clay, the colour and putrid smell arising from lack of air. Rainfall tended to run along the surface as much as sink in, my boots were covered in sticky mud for most of the winter, and then the soil capped hard in dry weather.

However, I dared to simply scrape out 5-7cm (2-3") of soil from 45cm (18") pathways on to 1.2m (4') beds, then to spread 5cm (2") or so of well-rotted horse manure on top of the slightly raised beds, which had no wooden sides. See page 39 for the pros and cons of sides for raised beds.

Clay soil like this grows good vegetables when mulched with compost and manure.

Adding the manure enabled worms and other soil life to reclaim the soil's health by reintroducing the air it was lacking. Looking at the abundant growth of verges and hedgerows, I could see that there was fertility in this soil. I just needed to help it happen again in the compacted soil. But how long would it take?

Vegetable growth in the first year was poor and made me realise how much the soil was suffering. I even wondered if I was doing the right thing, and was too embarrassed to take any photographs, much to my subsequent regret. I even dug one 20-metre section of bed where the soil seemed most compacted.

Then, in the second year of growing, after another autumnal application of horse manure and my own compost, harvests were on the good side of average. Most impressively, some parsnips grew fat and long. Vegetables on the dug section of bed were no larger or better than on the undug bed next to it.

Thereafter this plot of previously moribund soil has been growing an abundance of wonderful vegetables (see picture, right). On average there is a slight improvement every year, as I am still applying an inch or two (3-5cm) of compost and manure every autumn or winter, to beds only, on about two-thirds of the total area. Carrots and parsnips are sown into this tilth of organic matter and they grow superbly.

Creating a tilth

Here we come to the most obvious difference between digging and not digging and, if you are used to a soil tilth, it is the trickiest aspect to master. When organic matter is on the surface, all seeds and plants are sown or planted into it. Before doing this we need to help it break up into a suitably crumbly state, especially for small seeds.

- **Firstly,** it is best to use well-rotted manure and compost, of a dark brown colour and

Previously moribund soil made healthy with organic matter on top – compacted clay aerated by soil life.

not too soggy, preferably spread a month or two before sowing and planting. For quick results, fine materials such as mushroom and green waste compost can be applied and sown or planted into straight away if need be.

- **Secondly, aim to spread compost and manure in autumn or winter** as soon as the previous year's harvests have been taken. Or even, as we shall see later, around a winter harvest that is still waiting to happen. Doing this ensures that air can enter the organic matter, and weather combinations of frost, wetting and drying will tend to open up any clods, which can then be broken down with a raking across the surface, or by knocking with a fork.
- **Thirdly,** how much compost and manure to spread? I find that 3-5cm (1-2") every year works well on beds: I spread this depth of compost on about three-quarters of the beds' area, allowing birds to scatter it more widely over the following months.

Compost and manure on the surface

If you are used to digging and burying all additions of organic matter, this aspect of no-dig probably seems the strangest, in that you hardly ever see your soil until perhaps late summer, when worms have taken in most of the compost. There are great benefits to having dark, soft humus on top:

- It absorbs and retains moisture.
- It reduces cracking of the topsoil in dry weather.
- Its dark colour soaks up the spring sunshine to help warm the soil, so earlier growth is possible.
- It is much less sticky than dug soil.
- You have access in all weathers, without planks, because of the stable structure that develops underneath the dark, surface layer.

Also, there is a mulching effect on any weed seeds in the soil surface. After existing weeds have been dealt with using the methods described here, and as long as you pull out or hoe off all weeds that emerge, an undug soil becomes beautifully clean. I could never have time to grow and pick all the vegetables I produce without the weed-discouraging aspect of no-dig gardening. In the process pictured below, there were almost no weeds by the end.

Soil is alive!

Think of soil as a living organism that needs to recover after being disturbed and that is upset by digging or rotovating. The word 'recover' has two different meanings and they both apply here: after being disturbed, soil re-covers itself with weeds, and the presence of weeds helps it recover in a general way, returning to a healthy state.

Burying weeds

As a result of the mulching and no-dig effects, a well-run, undug plot has fewer weeds than a dug one. It becomes possible to keep the soil relatively weed free at all times and the question of needing to bury weeds with an autumn digging, or chop them up with a spring rotovation, does not arise.

On the other hand, if you inherit a weedy allotment or want to grow vegetables on a lawn or piece of pasture, there is a choice between an initial cultivation or mulching to exclude light. The latter takes rather longer but usually leaves the soil cleaner.

Cleaning weedy soil

There are three different stages to pass through when using mulches to reclaim weedy soil for growing vegetables.

1. **An initial composting and/or mulch of weedy and grassy plots.** Spreading some compost or manure is good for all vegetables and if you have enough, a 15cm (6") layer is sufficient on its own to smother and kill grass and many perennial weeds. This is not needed every year but just as a one-off application to weedy soil – see 'Making raised beds', page 38.

   Thinner layers of compost will need a light-excluding mulch on top, which could be cardboard, paper or black plastic of some kind. If cardboard is used on perennial weeds such as dandelions, couch grass and bindweed, a second layer will be needed after about ten weeks, as holes start to appear when cardboard stays wet, and perennial weeds can quickly recover unless they are kept totally in the dark until all reserves in their roots are

Mulching
1. Grass and pasture weeds, with some cow manure spread on top in late July.
2. Now covered with a mulch of paper.
3. Six weeks later, some paper has blown off.
4. Re-covering the damaged paper with cardboard.
5. In March another layer of cardboard is added. A row of raspberries has been planted in the middle.
6. By June the raspberries are growing and four plants of winter squash have been set out, with some compost spread on top of the cardboard.
7. August, a year after the initial mulching.

exhausted. Paper and cardboard mulches can be left in place to degrade and be taken in by worms, but plastic mulches are mostly not biodegradable and need removing before sowing – although you can plant vegetables such as courgettes and tomatoes through them if weeds are still dying underneath.

2. **Extra weeding.** The first year of growing often demands more weeding than subsequent years. Perennials that do re-grow, even after a long period of mulching, need careful trowelling out. Also, if only small amounts of compost have been spread on the surface, there may be a flush of annual weeds to hoe or pull at some point.

3 **Easy gardening.** Thereafter, fewer weeds need regular removal and it takes much less time. The key is to remove weeds little and often. A weed is a weed however big it is – pull it when small and keep your plot clean. This approach means no weeds going to seed, so you enter a virtuous circle of enjoyably clean soil, apart from weed seeds blowing in.

Clean, healthy soil, the promised land for all gardeners, is also maintained by an annual application of 3-5cm (1-2"), of reasonably well-rotted compost or animal manure. Soil kept healthy by a thin layer of organic matter on top has less need to grow weeds, as long as the applied compost is reasonably clean of weed seeds (see Chapter 4).

Deal with large perennial weeds

* Sometimes it is more practical to dig out perennial weeds such as brambles, nettles and docks, and any woody plants, which often look more dramatic than they really are. Their roots are not particularly invasive and do not re-grow when small pieces are left in the soil, unlike bindweed, marestail and ground elder.

Increasing fertility

Soil fertility is partly soil life, partly nutrients. The best growth happens when abundant soil life is able to make nutrients available for plants whenever they are needed.

Organic versus synthetic nutrients

Vegetables are hungry plants but this does not mean that you have to reach for a packet of artificial fertiliser. Some people ask if there is any difference between nutrients in 'chemical' or 'organic' form, but this is really the wrong question. We should actually be asking how stable and soluble the nutrients are.

- Nutrients in composts and well-rotted manures are mostly insoluble in water, so

Kale in early August after carrots. Some cow manure was spread on the soil before planting.

Summary of no-dig

- The beneficial inhabitants of undisturbed soil can proliferate more readily, leading to an increase of bacteria, fungi, mites, springtails, worms, beetles and so forth.
- The development of soil life helps a stable, firm yet open structure to develop, which can take the weight of a person or wheelbarrow without being compacted.
- Plant roots can penetrate easily into this stable structure, while also being well anchored.
- Much of the increased soil life provides food for plants as it decays.
- Fungi called mycorrhizae proliferate in undug soil and help many plants to find the nutrients they need, by serving as root elongations, in return for energy from the growing roots via photosynthesis in the plants' leaves.

rain does not wash them away into groundwater and streams, unlike most artificial fertilisers. This is better for the environment as well as for the garden.

- Nutrients from organic matter, after being stabilised by the processes of composting and/or decay, are generally present in balanced combinations for new growth. They become available when rising soil temperature allows roots to use them, resulting in steady, healthy growth of fine-tasting plants.
- The presence of nutrients in soil does not automatically mean that plant roots can reach and use them. What is needed is a soil structure that allows roots to reach the nutrients, and soil life that enables roots to use them. No-dig, with some organic matter on top, meets these requirements extremely well.

A lot of organic matter?

Because the organic matter in a no-dig garden is initially on top, it can look as though one is using more than in a dug garden. In fact, the amounts I use and recommend are, I believe, correct for all vegetable growing, to ensure the continuing health of soil, crops and people. Unfortunately, the advent of artificial fertilisers has encouraged gardeners to forget many highly worthwhile and traditional skills to do with looking after soil.

As recently as the beginning of the twentieth century, nearly all soil for growing vegetables was regularly fed with a rich combination of animal and human manures. Many old kitchen gardens still have deep, black soil as a result of this. The benefits last a lot longer than when synthetic nutrients are used.

Another way of looking at it is that, instead of digging, which does not increase fertility, you can spend the same amount of time in sourcing, making and spreading organic matter, which is improving the soil every year.

Soil qualities

Much also depends on the soil you are growing in, as some soils are by nature more fertile.

- **Clays and silts** have probably the best store of nutrients, at the same time being the most difficult to 'work'. This makes them excellent candidates for a no-dig approach, as in my current gardens and also in a previous one in France, where I produced excellent vegetables from some desperately difficult and unappealing white clay.
- **Stony soils.** By way of contrast, I cut my teeth on a Cotswold brash soil whose qualities are quite different – free-draining, stony and crumbly. No-dig worked well on

this lighter soil and stones were less troublesome on the surface than if the soil had been cultivated. Digging and tilling soil tends to bring stones to the surface.

- **Light and sandy soils** are perhaps the most difficult for growing vegetables because they can easily become short of both nutrients and moisture. Using larger amounts of slightly less rotted compost can help to retain moisture, and is not associated with the slug problems that this can lead to on heavy soils.

Fertility for winter crops

Little specific extra soil preparation is needed for growing winter vegetables, although for those that are sown or planted as second crops from July to September some extra organic matter may be needed, as in the photo of kale on page 36, where a harvest of carrots had already been taken.

When you manage to spread an inch or two (3-5cm) of compost or manure on beds in the autumn, this is sufficient for most soils to grow healthy vegetables throughout the following year. The exception is when a first crop of hungry brassicas, such as early cabbage and cauliflower, is grown for harvesting in June. A second planting of carrots, leeks and many other vegetables is then possible, but a thin extra layer of organic matter will often be worthwhile after early brassicas.

One of my beds of undug clay: although dense, the soil is crumbly, with worms at 40cm (16") deep.

Soil acidity

The question of soil acidity frequently arises and, although it matters, I advise those posing the question to pay more attention to general soil health than to a pH number. Most vegetables tolerate a wide range of acidity, from slightly acid to slightly alkaline, and changes in pH mostly have rather subtle effects, like less scab on potatoes in acid soil and slightly better brassicas in alkaline soil. For acid soils, adding lime occasionally may be beneficial, but this is mostly when compost and manure is in short supply.

Check this by observing how much of the autumn compost has been taken in by early summer. If none is visible at that time, spread just an inch (2-3cm) or so before planting or sowing again. Or you can plant a second crop, such as leeks, beetroot, cauliflower or chard, then spread some compost around the plants a fortnight or so later, once they are established. It depends on when you have some compost available, and enough time to spread it.

Making raised beds

Having always enjoyed great success with growing on raised beds, accessed from permanent paths between, I have been encouraged to see so many gardeners adopting this method over the last few years. Raised beds are productive, easy to manage and lend themselves well to a no-dig approach.

This lovely compost is a year old. It was covered to keep it dry, then sieved to use in potting.

1. Bed sides, or not

Raised beds can be contained by lengths of wood or recycled plastic. This keeps them tidy and makes a more easily maintained edge, helping to prevent invasion of the growing area by nearby grass and weeds. Sides can be any height you like: the most usual and useful is about 15cm (6"), which is tall enough to hold enough compost to mulch grass and most weeds – see right.

On the other hand, bed sides can allow soil to dry out more at the edges than in the middle and they can also harbour slugs and wood-lice, just enough to cause damage in damp weather.

Beds with sides

To convert a piece of lawn or a weedy area into a raised bed for growing vegetables, simply assemble the sides and ends on top of the weedy soil, then fill it with organic matter.

Sides of 15cm (6") hold enough material to deprive existing grass and weeds of light, so that they die within about three months on average. Then the soil they were growing in becomes available to your vegetables, in addition to the organic matter on top.

Aim to use reasonably well-rotted compost and manure, keeping the finest materials for the top layer, which you can sow or plant into as soon as the bed is made.

Beds without sides

Sides are not obligatory, and they become expensive when many beds are created on a large plot. Most of my beds have no fixed sides and are also only slightly raised, which helps conserve moisture.

I aim to have a growing area of beds that are raised just enough that I can clearly see them in contrast to the paths, so there is a gently undulating terrain of paths and beds (see photo on page 41). There are two ways to make beds like this, starting with flat ground.

- If the soil is clean of weeds, use a string to mark out 45cm (18") pathways and 1.2m (4') beds.
- Then run a sharp spade horizontally through the pathway soil to a depth of no

After filling

✻ Important: tread the bed ingredients down firmly after filling so that roots have a firm anchor. This also helps with moisture retention.

Beds can be made at any time of year: this one was created in February. A wooden frame was placed on the grass and weeds of an old pasture, then filled with compost. The experimental cardboard at one end made no difference.

more than 10cm (4") and put this soil on the bed, then rake it level.

- Some compost could then be spread on top of the bed, creating beds about 15cm (6") higher than the pathways.
- Or, where weeds are growing and you want to mulch them, spread compost and manure on top of the area that is to become beds, then cover all the plot, including pathways, with your chosen mulch (cardboard or black polythene) as described on page 35. These beds are then as high as the amount of organic matter you used.

2. Bed height

Beds can be as high or as low as you like, time and money permitting. Older gardeners or anyone with a stiff back may find high beds really helpful, but they are a lot of work to create. Low beds are easier to maintain.

My beds are higher in winter after compost has been spread, then lower in summer after blackbirds have scattered some of it into the pathways, which I don't mind because the paths' soil is a valuable resource for plants, and compost on paths conserves moisture.

3. Establishing and maintaining paths

Do pathways need to be mulched, and if so, with what materials? My experience has led me to the firm opinion that in larger plots such as allotments it is worth treating paths in the same way as beds – keep them thoroughly weeded, and even spread some rough compost on them, to maintain fertility and make weeding easier.

The difficult bit can be clearing paths of weeds in the first place. If you are starting with a weedy plot that contains perennials such as couch grass, a year of permanent

Keeping paths clean

Clean and fertile paths give an increased growing area, because vegetables can root into them. Roots of Swiss chard and courgettes, for example, can even travel through paths and into the next bed. In moist weather I notice lots of fine roots just under the path surfaces from vegetables such as salads, leeks and brassicas.

Late February: these beds were mulched with compost and manure in December. They are only slightly raised above path level: in spring some of this manure is flicked into pathways by blackbirds.

mulching may be needed to clear most of this, before establishing beds and paths.

An exception can be if you have enough space to create beds with sides, and wide enough paths between them for a rotary mower to keep the grass short. But grass is greedy and invasive so should never be allowed in pathways between shallow beds with no defined sides.

4. Maintaining productivity of beds

After filling a bed and firming down its compost and manure, it is perhaps hard to imagine that the contents will need topping up within a year. But they do settle, because organic matter is continually being incorporated into soil and reduces in volume when eaten by soil organisms. After a year's cropping, you will find that 15cm (6") of ingredients have become 10-12cm (4-5"). So I recommend an annual refilling to maintain beds in a full state.

If you don't, harvests will slowly decrease. Also, you will increasingly be bending down more. Compost can be put on at any time of year, whenever there is room to do so.

Growing on flat ground

If you don't like a system of beds and paths, it is still possible to grow without digging. I recently came across an inspiring book called *Successful Gardening Without Digging* by James Gunston, published in 1960 (see Resources).

One difference between his approach and mine was a greater emphasis on continual loosening of his heavy soil with a three-pronged hoe, which I think results from using less compost than I do, and shows that you can be successful with smaller inputs. But it seems that more work is then necessary during the growing season, dealing with weeds and crumbling the topsoil. Another aspect of Gunston's gardening was using space between growing crops to start following ones, known as inter-sowing.

This and other ways of increasing harvests are invaluable for having enough vegetables in winter, and there are many examples included in Chapter 5.

Chapter 4

Making your own compost

Transforming waste into something really healthy

Few aspects of gardening invite a playful approach as much as compost making. Have one or two goes and you will start to enjoy the possibilities, all crowned by the final moment of opening a heap to see the goodness it contains – or sometimes not! All heaps have a different final quality, often with room for improvement. Read through the descriptions on the following pages to see what you can do, then enjoy it – making compost is as creative and interesting as growing plants.

Your precious compost has two important roles:

1. It is a health inoculant for the garden, meaning that small quantities can make a dramatic difference to soils that have been poorly treated and are lacking in living organisms.
2. It is a source of nutrients that are not leached by rain because they are held by humus in a stable form. This means that compost, and also composted manure, *can safely be spread in autumn and winter* without fear of its nutrients being washed out by rain – which happens outside the growing season to water-soluble artificial fertilisers.

Spreading compost on the surface of your beds allows it to be absorbed at the soil's own speed; there is no need to damage soil life through mechanical incorporation. Annual applications, of anything from 1cm to 5cm (½-2"), enable a healthy, dark layer of fertile topsoil to develop gradually, resulting in better plant growth every year.

Compost ingredients

Some ingredients compost more readily than others. Most heaps are assembled with whatever comes to hand, which varies through the seasons and is seldom a perfect formulation for making compost. However, results can be improved by a few little changes, such as adding some fresh animal droppings and mixing dry ingredients with soggy ones.

The size of ingredients is a critical factor in influencing the speed of composting. Shredding or chopping gives small pieces that rot

Right: Compost heaps are mostly dormant in winter, but this robin is hoping for a worm.

This compost, mostly from garden waste and grass, was started in April. Here it is being spread in October.

more quickly. On the other hand, too much fine matter, such as grass mowings, can compact and exclude air. It's good to include many different ingredients of varied sizes, added in batches over time.

Moisture is a critical ingredient – neither too little nor too much. If possible, add dry and really wet ingredients at the same time. Dry materials in large quantities will need some watering, but most compost ingredients are sufficiently moist.

Other ingredients

- **Animal manures,** for example, chicken and hamster droppings, are valuable in small quantities to bring stimulating organisms and extra nutrients to the heap. They are a kind of activator, helping heaps to develop the right balance of bacteria and fungi. Urine has a similar role. You can also use commercial formulations such as 'Quick Return' (QR) herbal powder or biodynamic preparations (see BDAA in Resources).
- **Soil** is sometimes recommended as an ingredient, but there is usually quite enough on roots of plants, and too much soil results in a cooler, less active heap.
- **Lime** is often advocated but is definitely not needed if the soil is high in pH (chalk or limestone soils), and even when soil is acid there is a mysterious alchemy in composting that tends to raise pH, without any use of lime.

What to include in a heap

Anything that once grew can be composted, even if processed into newspaper, starch cups or cellulose credit cards, although the last two are slow to decompose. Metal, glass and synthetic materials based on plastic will not decompose in domestic compost heaps.

It can help to think of a compost heap's ingredients as being either 'green' or 'brown', in terms of adding and mixing them to have more success in composting.

Green: all fresh green matter – weeds (with as little soil as possible), grass mowings, fresh leafy prunings and kitchen waste. These provide heat but need brown material as well to prevent sogginess.

Brown: all woody organic matter – twigs, newspaper, cardboard, dead leaves, straw. These decompose slowly and provide structure to maintain aerated conditions, and are also important food for a range of bacteria and fungi.

It is important to achieve a good balance of 'greens' and 'browns'. A balance of half green and half brown is good, and two-thirds green to one-third brown is a fair compromise, achievable in summer. In winter there is often too little green, which results in cooler, slow composting.

A layer of old straw (brown) being spread over a layer of cleared salad plants (green) in late October; the straw helps to hold air in the heap.

- **Seaweed** and **rockdust** (the latter available from the SEER Centre – see Resources) can be added in small amounts to provide minerals. You can also add some **wood ash** and **dust bags** of vacuum cleaners if they contain no plastic (unlikely!).

Can diseased plants be composted?

Diseased material is often compostable as few plant diseases survive the process, even in a cool heap. In Britain at least, tomatoes and potatoes with blight can safely be composted, because blight arrives on the wind rather than overwintering in soil. But a few organisms – for instance, the main fungal diseases of alliums – will survive composting, so I advise burning any onions, leeks or garlic that are infected with white rot, and onions with mildew (see pages 86-7).

Composting roots of perennial weeds

Roots of perennial weeds such as bindweed, docks, couch grass and dandelions can all be successfully composted as long as there are enough other ingredients to enable a combination of darkness and warm or hot composting to break them down. Put them in the middle of a heap if its sides are exposed to light, to prevent them from re-growing out of the sides. They could also be killed and eventually broken down, over at least six months, in a bin (or a sack if need be) that excludes all light.

Composting weed seeds

Seeds are more tricky: hundreds of viable seeds on every weed that has set seed will be killed only in the centre of hot heaps, above about 50°C (122°F). This is most likely in the centre of heaps assembled over weeks rather than months, with about two-thirds green matter, and is difficult to achieve in most garden heaps.

When heaps are assembled more slowly, over many months, I recommend burning weeds that have set seed. Then see whether you can do your next weeding when the weeds are small, definitely before flowering, in order to be able to compost them cleanly.

Weeds germinating on this compost heap suggest it is ready for spreading.

Life in a compost heap

Bacteria are a key ingredient of successful compost heaps: their fast multiplication in warm, aerated conditions leads to considerable heat and rapid decomposition.

Fungi proliferate at lower temperatures and also in heaps dominated by brown waste, and are as vital as bacteria in helping decomposition. Many of them can live healthily in soil when compost is spread and are an important part of soil fertility.

Worms found in compost, when it is more decomposed, are mostly brandlings (*Eisenia foetida*): small, thin and bright red. They increase in the final, cooler stages – as long as heaps are mostly aerobic – and their excretions are beautiful black humus. When spread with compost, they mostly do not survive and, unlike earthworms (*Lumbricus terrestris*), they do not burrow in an important way, or eat large amounts of soil; their main value is in the compost heap.

In this four-month-old heap, ingredients are still unrotted at the sides but are starting to look brown towards the middle.

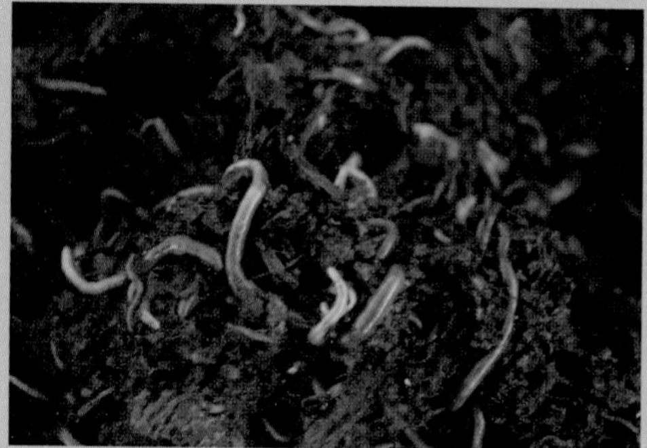

Many brandling worms were found at the bottom of this nine-month-old heap, eating the three-quarters-decomposed compost.

The composting process

No two heaps result in exactly the same compost. Here are some reasons why, and suggestions for a few ways of improving the finished product.

Air, moisture and turning

Air is necessary so that working organisms can breathe. Heaps with enough air are called aerobic, are of pleasant odour and result in soft, crumbly compost. Heaps with insufficient air, often caused by too much moisture, are called anaerobic and become unpleasant smelling and soggy.

Turning with a fork is a useful remedy for anaerobic heaps because it introduces air; turning in a sealed drum is less effective because oxygen is not entering. If you have the time and energy, turning a heap every week can result in near-perfect compost.

On the other hand, successful compost can be made without any turning – it just takes longer – around a year for the bottom of a heap that has been assembled slowly: see the picture on page 48.

Heap edges, size and covers

Heap bases may be soil, stone or concrete. I prefer soil, but a friend has great success with heaps on asphalt, and they even fill up with worms, which must come in as eggs in small lumps of soil.

Heap sides may be of wood, wire or plastic, preferably with gaps to allow some air to enter. Heaps can also be made without sides, but the outside ingredients will then compost more slowly.

A cover is not obligatory, but any cardboard, textile material or bin lid on top retains heat and still allows heaps to breathe. Polythene

This rough, mulch-quality material, made from grass mowings and straw, is not really compost.

An excellent bin, placed on soil: the compost at its bottom is a year old and ready to use.

works too – although it doesn't breathe, it excludes rain and that helps to keep air in.

For small gardens, plastic bins are tidy and hold heat fairly well. They tend to be airless, so be careful not to add too many green ingredients in one go. Conical bins are easy to lift off a mostly finished heap, for access to the final product. If the bin is then placed nearby it can be filled with the top layer of uncomposted material from the old heap, then you can spread the good compost from the base of the old heap on to your beds.

Larger gardens justify a heap of about 1.2m x 1.2m (4' x 4'). To make its sides, old pallets can simply be tied together at their corners. At least two heaps are needed, one to mature while another is being filled, and having three in one place makes it possible to turn one into the other at intervals.

Heap temperature

Heaps that are filled regularly will start off warm, become hot briefly or at intervals when green waste is added, then cool gradually over many months. In winter there is unlikely to be any heat because fresh green material is lacking and the air is too cold.

After rapid assembly of ingredients in the warmer months, with at least half green waste, temperatures of 65°C (149°F) are attainable within three days. This can result in finished compost within three to six months, especially if a heap is turned.

After the subsidence of heat there is a lukewarm stage when brandling worms start to arrive; they multiply fast in the last cooler stage, helping the final decomposition process. Their excretions are hugely fertile 'vermicompost' (see page 51).

However, composting can also succeed without heat. Cool or occasionally warm composting occurs when ingredients are in a small heap, or are gathered slowly, or are more brown than green, or are gathered in cold weather. No significant heat is maintained, but compost can be formed within a year in the heap's oldest part. Compared with hot compost there are often more worms, beetles, woodlice and other visible soil organisms, as well as more fungi than bacteria.

Tools

A sharp spade or knife are useful for cutting any stems and twigs into 10-15cm (4-6") lengths. A manure fork with long, thin prongs is good for turning and eventually spreading the heap.

Mechanical shredding is undoubtedly of great benefit, because smaller ingredients rot more quickly and evenly. But a shredder is energy intensive and most of us make fair compost without one. If so desired, shredding can be achieved by running a rotary lawnmower over small heaps of large or long ingredients, such as broad-bean stems and woody prunings, before adding them to a heap.

The final product

Good compost is dark brown or black, more crumbly than lumpy, and pleasant smelling; some residual woody ingredients are often still present and also some brandling worms.

Fully mature compost from older heaps, called humus, is a beautiful material. Its small dark lumps of organic matter are soft, light in weight, and of the highest value in adding permanent structure to soils.

By contrast, when compost has not finished maturing, for whatever reason, half or more of the original ingredients can still be recognised, perhaps with a smell of ammonia, indicating that bacteria are still working and meaning that you need to wait a little. Or there may be sulphurous methane, indicating a lack of air and a need to turn.

Compost cures

* **Slimy, smelly compost.** Thoroughly turn the heap and break up any large masses of material, then keep rain from entering it. In your next heap, add more brown ingredients.

* **Dry heaps with air pockets.** Turn the heap and chop up any larger ingredients, adding a little moisture if it is dry to the touch. Use a watering can with a fine rose so that moisture is spread evenly.

* **Heaps that never fill up.** The miracle of compost is making waste disappear, but you should still have some good material at the bottom. A smaller heap would perhaps work better for the amount of waste you have.

Compost teas

These are made from a small amount of high-quality humus in plenty of water, sometimes with the addition of molasses. A mechanical paddle is used for vigorous stirring and oxygenation over 24 hours, resulting in a massive multiplication of the initial bacteria and fungi.

The compost in the middle of this heap has broken down beautifully, under a less rotted surface – small pieces of wood have helped to keep air in the heap.

Teas are then sprayed on to leaves and watered on to soil. Their success in helping plants to grow is a vital clue in appreciating how compost is valuable for its *life qualities and organisms* as much as for its nutrients.

Buying compost and manure

Because vegetables are hungry plants and grow most healthily in humus-rich soil, you will probably wish to supplement your own compost by buying some in.

Animal manures

The richest composts are made from the manures of all animals, especially after being stacked in a heap for a year or so, with the right balance of bedding to give a good structure. Straw, paper and sawdust bedding result in better compost than wood shavings, which take longer to rot down.

The amount of nutrients in manure depends on the animal (of the common animals, chicken manure has the most and horse manure the least) and on the proportion of bedding.

Chemical residues

Manure from intensively farmed animals, such as battery hens and pigs, is likely to contain antibiotics and is best avoided. Of even greater concern is a long-lived herbicide, known as aminopyralid, which has recently been allowed for use on grassland. Unfortunately it is so persistent – having a weed-killing effect on grassland after 18 months – that some survives in the manure of animals that have eaten grass or hay that were sprayed with it. Sometimes you can find this out by asking a farmer, but horse owners who buy hay may not know if it is contaminated.

Most grassland is not sprayed with this weedkiller, so the risk of contamination is small. But I suggest you do a quality check by placing some of the manure in a box or seed tray, with some soil, then sow or plant tomatoes, salads or peas and beans. Keep the tray warm and light, then if growth is happening normally within two or three weeks, the manure is safe. Any contamination would cause leaves to curl upwards, in which case you should not buy or take delivery of this manure.

If you already have some contaminated manure, the only vegetables that will tolerate it are brassicas and sweetcorn; it can also be used around trees and soft fruit. But it is certainly something to avoid if at all possible.

Salads sown in two different batches of cow manure six weeks earlier, as a test for aminopyralid. Healthy growth indicates the manure is safe to use.

Bought composts

Bagged composts are of variable quality and may not be clearly labelled. I once bought a sack labelled 'organic farmyard manure', which looked like woody, green waste compost and grew very poor lettuce. It's best to experiment with just one sack and if you find a good product, stay with it. But bagged compost is an expensive way to improve soil.

Bagged animal manure, for example, pellets of dried chicken manure, is a form of concentrated nutrients, more than you find in compost. There should be instructions for use on the bag – don't spread them too thickly.

Green waste compost is usually black, crumbly and often contains many small pieces of woody material. Quality varies according to who made it and the different balance of ingredients. Nutrients are often in short supply at first, while the woody bits are decomposing, and this compost is best used as a bulking agent to help with moisture retention and aeration of soil: both are achieved by spreading it on top.

Mushroom compost has been used to grow a crop of mushrooms and is mostly straw, with some animal manure, peat and chalk, giving it a high pH. It improves for being composted for up to three months after you receive it.

Multipurpose compost is formulated with extra nutrients to grow plants in modules, pots and containers. It can be used to improve soil, at a cost and, unless organic, it contains water-soluble nutrients so should be spread only in the growing season when plants can take up nutrients before they are washed out.

Vermicompost is the result of organic matter being digested by worms and broken down by the bacteria in their guts. Soft, rich and of small volume, it is ideal for plant raising and container growing.

This mushroom compost was full of rotted but recognisable straw two months earlier in September, but has since broken down into a fine compost. You can also see small lumps of black peat, used in growing mushrooms.

Chapter 5

What to grow for winter

Planning a plot, with times of sowing and harvesting

Deciding what to grow

Although there are many reasons for growing one vegetable and not another, the main factor that should influence your decision is taste. Do you enjoy eating Brussels sprouts, swedes and parsnips? If not, grow leeks and salads, or other vegetables from the many that are possible for winter. However, I do recommend trying a few vegetables you have not liked before, because, when well grown and freshly harvested, they may taste better than you remember.

It also helps to be clear about which vegetables need to be stored and which ones are hardy enough to stay in the soil (see Part 5). In most parts of Britain November is a key month, when many vegetables need harvesting to store before the severe winter frosts arrive.

Frozen vegetables

Potatoes are destroyed by any freezing at all, yet can be stored for a long time in a cool but frost-free environment. On the other hand, onions and garlic tolerate being frozen and store best when dry. Part 5 has more information on this.

The vegetables most likely to grace your plot in winter are Brussels sprouts, savoy cabbage, corn salad (lamb's lettuce), kale, leaf beet, leeks, parsnips, rhubarb, spinach and swedes. Any of them can be harvested as needed, snow and heavy frost permitting. Salads are worth attempting but require protection for best results; this is covered in Part 6.

The two tables on pages 54-8 give a summary of best timings for growing outdoors (see Part 6 for growing under cover). These dates are guidelines that allow for some flexibility according to local conditions. Sowing and harvesting outside these times is possible in a few situations, which are described in the main text. Some of the vegetables listed in the tables can be sown at other times for harvests in summer and autumn.

Right: 'Doric F1' Brussels sprouts in December snow.

Winter vegetable calendar, outdoors			
Vegetable	**Sowing period⁺**	**Main harvest period**	**Storage period**
Asparagus	Feb–Mar (sow)* Mar–Apr (plants & crowns) or June–July (plants)	Apr–June	Eat fresh
Beans, broad	Oct–early Nov**	June–July	Eat fresh
Beans for drying	May*	Sept–Oct	2 years
Beetroot	May–June**	Oct–Dec	4-5 months
Broccoli, purple sprouting	May–early June	Mar–May	Eat fresh
Brussels sprouts	Apr–May	Oct–Apr	2 weeks
Cabbage, spring	Mid–late Aug	Apr–June	Eat fresh
Cabbage, winter (ballhead)	May	Oct–Nov	4-5 months, until Apr
Cabbage, winter (savoy)	May–June	Nov–Apr	2 weeks
Carrot	June**	Oct–Nov	4-5 months, until Apr
Cauliflower, spring	June–July	Mar–May	Eat fresh
Celeriac	Mar–early Apr*	Oct–Apr	Nov–Apr
Chard / leaf beet	July–early Aug**	Mar–May if mild winter	1 week
Chervil / coriander	Late July–Aug	Oct–Nov & Mar–Apr	1 week
Chicory (forcing)	May–1st week June	Nov	1 week
Chicory (heart)	July**	Oct–Dec	Nov–Jan
Chicory (leaf)	Late July–Aug**	Oct–May	1 week
Chinese cabbage	Late July*	Oct–Nov	Nov–Dec
Corn salad	Aug–Sept	Oct–Apr	1 week
Endive (heart)	Early Aug**	Oct–Dec	3 weeks, Nov–Dec
Endive (leaf)	Mid-Aug**	Oct–Nov & Mar–May	1 week
Garlic	Late Sept–early Oct	Late June–early July	July–May
Jerusalem artichoke	Mar–Apr	Oct–Apr	4 weeks
Kale	May–June	Oct–May	1 week
Land cress	Aug	Oct–Apr	1 week
Leek	Apr	Oct–Apr	4-6 weeks
Lettuce	Late Aug	Apr–June	1 week
Onion (bulb) / shallot	Jan–Mar (sow) Late Mar–Apr (sets/bulbs)	Late July–Aug	Aug–May

(Cont'd)

Vegetable	Sowing period+	Main harvest period	Storage period
Onion, salad	Late Aug**	Apr–June	1 week
Oriental leaves	Aug	Sept–Dec & Mar–May	1 week
Parsley	July–early Aug	Oct–Dec & Mar–May	1 week
Parsnip	Mar	Oct–Apr	Nov–Apr
Peas for shoots	Mar–Apr	May–June	Eat fresh
Potato, maincrop & second early	Mar–early May	Aug–Sept	Aug–Apr
Rhubarb	Mar–May (sow) May–June (plants) Nov–Dec (roots)	Mar–June	1 week
Rocket, salad	Late Aug	Oct–Dec & Mar–Apr	1 week
Rocket, wild	July–early Aug	Oct–Dec & Mar–June	1 week
Seakale	Mar–June (sow) Mar–Apr or May–June (plants)	Apr–May	1 week
Sorrel	Early Aug**	Oct–Dec & Mar–May	1 week
Spinach	Aug**	Oct–Dec & Mar–May	1 week
Squash, winter	Apr*	Oct	Oct–Apr
Swede	June*	Oct–Apr	Oct–Apr
Turnip / winter radish	Early Aug	Oct–Apr	3 months
Winter purslane	Aug	Oct–Dec & Mar–Apr	2 weeks

+ 'Sowing' includes planting for vegetables normally set out as sets and tubers, and perennials set out as plants. Except where indicated, dates are for sowing outdoors. See page 77 for indoor sowing dates.

* Best sown indoors.

** Note that these sowing dates are for winter harvests. Other sowing times are appropriate for harvests in other seasons.

The growing year

The table overleaf gives a month-by-month guide to which vegetables to sow, plant and harvest. There is something to do every month, especially if you grow a wide range. My suggestions for the month of sowing are flexible in spring, so you can sow parsnips in May if you have not managed to before, but in July and August, when the proximity of autumn means a rapid loss of growing time, I urge you to keep closely to these dates.

The harvesting descriptions apply to an 'average' winter of mixed weather. Long spells of unusually low temperatures and thick snow will reduce the outdoor harvests and make your stored vegetables more valuable, whereas in a mild winter there may be extra greens, leeks, turnips and other vegetables that are more marginal in extreme weather.

Any exceptions to the general guidelines in the table overleaf are given in the detailed entries for each vegetable in Parts 3 and 4.

Winter vegetables outdoors, month by month			
Month	**Sow⁺**	**Plant**	**Harvest**
March	Asparagus*, celeriac*, onion/shallot, parsnip, rhubarb, seakale*	Asparagus crowns & plants, Jerusalem artichoke, onion sets & plants / shallot bulbs, potato, seakale	Beetroot, Brussels sprouts, celeriac, chard / leaf beet, chervil, chicory (leaf & forcing), coriander, corn salad, endive (leaf), Jerusalem artichoke, kale, land cress, leek, parsley, parsnip, purple sprouting broccoli, rhubarb, rocket (salad & wild), spinach, spring cabbage, spring cauliflower, sorrel, swede, turnip, winter cabbage (savoy), winter purslane
April	Brussels sprouts, celeriac (early April)*, leek, parsnip, rhubarb, seakale, winter squash*	Asparagus crowns & plants, Jerusalem artichoke, onion sets & plants / shallot bulbs, potato, seakale	Asparagus, beetroot, Brussels sprouts, celeriac, chard / leaf beet, chervil, chicory (leaf & forcing), coriander, corn salad, endive (leaf), Jerusalem artichoke, kale, land cress, leek, parsley, parsnip, purple sprouting broccoli, rhubarb, rocket (salad & wild), seakale, sorrel, spinach, spring cabbage, spring cauliflower, swede, turnip, winter cabbage (savoy), winter purslane
May	Beans for drying, beetroot, Brussels sprouts, chicory (forcing), kale, parsnip, purple sprouting broccoli, rhubarb, winter cabbage (ballhead)	Beans for drying, celeriac, potato (early May), rhubarb, seakale, winter squash	Asparagus, bean tops, chard / leaf beet, chicory (leaf), endive (leaf), green garlic, lettuce, parsley, purple sprouting broccoli, rhubarb, salad onion, seakale, sorrel, spinach, spring cabbage, spring cauliflower, wild rocket
June	Beans for drying, beetroot, carrot, kale, purple sprouting broccoli*, spring cauliflower, swede*, winter cabbage (savoy)	Beans for drying, Brussels sprouts, celeriac, chicory for forcing, kale, leek, purple sprouting broccoli, rhubarb, seakale, winter cabbage (ballhead & savoy), winter squash (early June)	Asparagus, broad beans, spring cabbage, garlic, lettuce, rhubarb, salad onion, spinach, wild rocket
July	Carrot, chard / leaf beet, chervil, chicory (heart & leaf), Chinese cabbage*, coriander, endive (heart), parsley, sorrel, spring cauliflower, wild rocket	Beetroot, kale, leek, purple sprouting broccoli, spring cauliflower, swede, winter cabbage (savoy)	Garlic, broad beans, shallot

(Cont'd)

Month	Sow+	Plant	Harvest
August (first half)	Chard / leaf beet, chicory (leaf), chervil, coriander, endive (heart), land cress, oriental leaves, parsley, sorrel, spinach, turnip, wild rocket, winter purslane, winter radish	Chard / leaf beet, chicory (heart & leaf), Chinese cabbage, leaf beet, sorrel	Onion, potato
August (second half)	Corn salad, endive (leaf), land cress, oriental leaves, salad onion, salad rocket, spinach, spring cabbage, lettuce, winter purslane	Chicory (leaf), chervil, coriander, endive (heart & leaf), land cress, oriental leaves, parsley, rocket (salad & wild), sorrel, spinach, winter purslane	Potato
September	Corn salad, oriental leaves, salad onion, green manures, winter salads	Chervil, coriander, corn salad, endive (heart & leaf), garlic, land cress, lettuce, oriental leaves, parsley, salad onion, spinach, spring cabbage, winter purslane	Beans for drying (late September), potato
October	Broad beans	Garlic	Beans for drying, beetroot, Brussels sprouts, carrot, celeriac, chervil, chicory (heart), Chinese cabbage, coriander, corn salad, endive (heart & leaf), Jerusalem artichoke, kale, land cress, leek, oriental leaves, parsley, parsnip, rocket, spinach, sorrel, swede, turnip, winter cabbage (ballhead), winter purslane, winter radish, winter squash
November	Broad beans (early November)	Garlic if not already planted, rhubarb	Beetroot, Brussels sprouts, carrot, celeriac, chervil, chicory (heart, leaf & root for forcing), Chinese cabbage, coriander, corn salad, endive (heart & leaf), Jerusalem artichoke, kale, land cress, leek, oriental leaves, parsley, parsnip, rocket, spinach, sorrel, swede, turnip, winter cabbage (ballhead & savoy), winter purslane & radish
December		Rhubarb	Beetroot, Brussels sprouts, celeriac, chard / leaf beet, corn salad, chicory ((heart, leaf & root for forcing), endive (leaf), Jerusalem artichoke, kale, land cress, leek, oriental leaves, parsley, parsnip, rocket (salad & wild), spinach, swede, turnip, winter cabbage (savoy), winter purslane

(Cont'd)

Month	Sow+	Plant	Harvest
January	Onion/shallot*		Beetroot, Brussels sprouts, celeriac, chicory (chicons), corn salad, Jerusalem artichoke, kale, land cress, leek, parsnip, swede, turnip, winter cabbage (savoy), winter purslane
February	Onion/shallot*		Beetroot, Brussels sprouts, winter cabbage (savoy), celeriac, chicory (chicons), corn salad, Jerusalem artichoke, kale, land cress, leek, parsnip, purple sprouting broccoli, swede, turnip, winter purslane

+ Except where indicated, dates are for sowing outdoors. See page 77 for indoor sowing dates.
* Best sown indoors.

Main season & second-crop vegetables

Vegetables mature at vastly different speeds. It helps to divide them into main and second crops, where the main crops need most time to grow, and second crops can be sown or planted later in summer after another vegetable has already been grown in that soil.

Some vegetables fall into both categories: leeks and kale can be planted earlier or later, depending how large you want them to grow and when you want a harvest.

This rocket (front) was sown on 13 August and planted after peas on 2 September, while the carrots (behind) were sown late, on 16 July.

The same rocket in late October after many leaves have been picked and after some slight frosts; the carrots are now small to medium size.

Growth of overwintered garlic, and its harvesting on 1 July, followed by planting of brassicas for winter on the same day

1. Garlic was planted in October and is growing strongly by March. Only a little weeding has been needed because the soil is clean.
2. Using a trowel to harvest the fine bulbs of garlic on 1 July.
3. After the garlic, winter brassicas are planted and watered in, then covered with mesh.
4. The same bed in September. Purple sprouting broccoli and kale are now growing healthily.

Main-season vegetables for winter

The main-season vegetables are Brussels sprouts, celeriac, parsnips, maincrop potatoes and winter squash. They all need to be in place between March and early June, so there is little time to grow anything before them. Bulb onions are normally grown as a single crop, but their harvest time in early August actually allows time for a second vegetable – for example, turnips can be sown or endives planted after they are removed.

Most main-season plants require plenty of room to grow, so I would hesitate to plant Brussels sprouts, maincrop potatoes or winter squash in a small space. You can check this by referring to the spacings given in the individual plant entries in Part 3 – compare the average distance between plants with the size of your beds and plot. The figures in Part 3 are a blend of row and plant spacings: exact distances depend on whether you grow in wide rows with room for walking between, or on beds with closer and more equal spacings.

Winter vegetables as second crops

There are plenty of possible combinations of first and second crops, and the list in the table below gives some of the many choices. It is a good idea to plan ahead and be prepared with plants or seeds, because second crops need every bit of time in their part-season's growing to reach a worthwhile size before winter.

As an example, when the last carrots of a spring sowing are pulled, this is the procedure:

1. The bed is cleared of any weeds.
2. The soil and compost is firmed if it has become loose from harvesting the carrots.
3. Seed is sown or the next crop of leeks, kale, autumn salads or whatever is then planted straight away.
4. In dry weather, any drills are watered before sowing and plants are watered in after planting.

Using raised plants

* More success with second cropping comes when you propagate or buy plants rather than sowing direct. The second-crop plants can even be planted on the same day as a previous harvest is finished.

Second crops sometimes require a little extra compost, depending on how much you applied the previous autumn or winter. I usually find that my autumn dressing is sufficient, with some lingering remains of dark humus on the surface through summer, but if

Some examples of winter vegetables as second crops

First vegetable	Second vegetable
Beans, broad, sown November	Leek from plants sown in April; kale
Beans, broad, sown March/April	Oriental leaves
Beans, runner or climbing French	Garlic
Beetroot sown indoors March	Endive, chicory, swede, kale
Beetroot sown outdoors April	Turnip, oriental leaves
Cabbage, spring, overwintered	Leek as above; potato – many possible
Calabrese sown indoors March	Lettuce, endive, chicory, corn salad
Carrot sown late March/April	Leek, spinach
Dwarf (French) beans	Cabbage (spring), corn salad
Lettuce sown indoors February	Purple sprouting broccoli, cabbage (winter), swede
Lettuce sown outdoors April	Kale, oriental leaves, turnip
Onion sown March, planted April	Kale, winter radish, land cress
Peas sown late March/April	Beetroot, carrot, salads
Potato, early	Carrot, leek, purple sprouting broccoli, swede
Potato, second early	Oriental leaves
Spinach sown March/April	Many possible, even celeriac

it has all been taken in by worms and there is some good compost to hand, you can spread half an inch or so (1cm) around the new plants, either before the second planting/sowing or afterwards.

An example of winter vegetables as second crops

Here is a season's cropping I did in 2008 on one undug bed of 1.4m x 2.5m (5' x 8'), to give an idea of how to use a space fully and for most of the time. In this case, the winter vegetables were harvested by late November and stored. This bed received a surface dressing of 5cm (2") of home-made compost in December. Frost then opened up any lumps in the compost and it was raked to a medium tilth, not especially fine.

I planted and sowed in rows across the beds, clearing and replanting some at different times. The following is a plan for the whole season, and the timings. Where plants were used, they were raised in modules in my greenhouse.

Calendar

Mid-March Sow two rows of parsnips with one row of radishes between. Sow spinach, plant onion sets, early potato tubers and lettuce; cover beds with fleece.

Late April-May Harvest radishes, spinach and lettuce leaves.

May Clear remains of flowering spinach and plant celeriac (sown in March indoors).

June Harvest more lettuce and early potatoes.

July Plant swedes (from sowing indoors in early June); harvest onions; remove flowering lettuce and plant red cabbage by mid-month.

August Plant endive and radicchio by mid-month.

October and/or November Depending on frost, harvest red cabbage, endive, radicchio and celeriac.

October onwards Harvest parsnips and swedes.

Harvests

Of the winter vegetables that interest us here, the harvests were as follows. The following year's winter harvests are also mentioned, to emphasise how they can vary!

Onions only 0.9kg because of mildew. (6kg in 2009, for various reasons; see pages 86-7).

Red cabbage 2.6kg hearts from four plants (0.2kg in 2009 due to gall midge; see box, page 103).

April. From left: parsnips with radishes sown between; spinach, lettuce and onion; early potatoes out of the picture on the right.

The same beds in October: parsnips still, celeriac (after spinach), red cabbage (after lettuce), endive (after onion), swedes (after potatoes).

Celeriac 2.5kg from four plants (4.3kg in 2009).
Parsnips 6kg (9.7kg in 2009).
Swedes 3.3kg (not grown in 2009, carrots in 2009 0.8kg).
(1kg = 2lb 3oz)

The bed's harvest of winter vegetables was 15.3kg and its total yield over the season was 27.2kg. In 2009 the same bed yielded 21kg of winter vegetables; 30.1kg altogether, reflecting a difference in weather and also in crop choices.

Vegetable rotation

Please do not let this section discourage you from growing vegetables! Rotation is less important, especially in small gardens, than is often portrayed. Don't worry if your rotation is not classically correct – I know that mine isn't – but it is worth respecting the principles as far as possible, for better soil and plant health.

All vegetables of the brassica family: wild rocket, land cress, and red and green pak choi.

Rotation means growing vegetables from the same family in a different place each year. It is a sound idea, but its application has become dogmatic. It needs thinking through for a result that is most suited to each garden and plot, and should be viewed mainly as a guideline.

Vegetable *families* are a botanical distinction: for instance, brassicas include such varied vegetables as cabbage, mizuna and turnips. In terms of rotation it makes no sense to talk of 'roots' or 'salads' because they belong to many families: celeriac belongs to the umbellifers and potato to the solanums.

The aim is to keep a reasonable period of time between growing vegetables of the same family. This is to prevent the pests and diseases that are specific to each family from establishing in any quantity.

However, most advice on rotation assumes that one vegetable crop is grown every year. Yet it is possible and also desirable, as discussed above, to grow a second crop wherever an opportunity arises. This makes a four-year rotation impossible to practise, as you would then need to regularly eat vegetables from six or seven groups or families.

This leads to the other problem with fixed rotations: the allocation of rigid areas for groups of vegetables – one quarter potatoes, one quarter brassicas, etc. – when few people want to consume those proportions of food, and the seeds or plants we have may not fit into exactly this area.

I suggest you become familiar with the list of family groupings shown on the right, then use it to make some rough plans of what you might grow where, including your second sowings and plantings of the year. The list includes summer as well as winter vegetables, with commonly used 'family' names in brackets at the end of some groups.

Think about what you want

* In smaller gardens especially, it makes more sense to start off by deciding what you like to eat, then work out an approximate rotation based on groupings of plant families. I say 'approximate' because a few plants or sowings may fail and need replacing, sometimes with different ones, depending on what is available, and when.

Notice how salad plants come from many different families, so if you wish to grow only salad it is possible to devise a rotation of sorts, around groups of brassicas, compositae, umbellifers, legumes, the odd allium and other smaller groups.

Do bear in mind that rotation is most practical in larger plots. In polytunnels, it is difficult to have more than two years between crops.

Winter vegetables in containers

Containers are less suitable for winter vegetables than for summer ones, due to the one-off nature of so many winter harvests. This means a lot of effort and compost for relatively little return, compared with salad leaves or tomatoes.

Also there is the question of frost and whether containers will stand their compost being frozen and expanded, as well as how the vegetables will survive.

A good way of using large pots and containers for winter-harvest vegetables is to grow plants 'halfway' in them, then plant the semi-mature kale, cabbage and leeks in September into beds vacated by tomatoes, courgettes and

Vegetable plant families

Apiaceae/Umbelliferae: bulb (florence) fennel, carrot, celery, celeriac, chervil, coriander, dill, mitsuba, parsley, parsnip, sweet cicely (umbellifers)

Asteraceae/Compositae: globe and Jerusalem artichoke, cardoon, chicory, endive, lettuce, salsify, scorzonera, sunflower, tansy, tarragon (compositae)

Brassicaceae/Cruciferae: broccoli, Brussels sprouts, cabbage, calabrese, Chinese cabbage, kale, kohlrabi, land cress, mibuna, mizuna, mustard, pak choi, radish, rape, rocket, seakale, swede, tatsoi, turnip, watercress (brassicas)

Chenopodiaceae: beetroot, chard, leaf beet, orache, spinach (beets)

Cucurbitaceae: courgette, cucumber, gherkin, melon, pumpkin, squash, watermelon (cucurbits)

Fabaceae/Leguminosae: asparagus peas, broad beans, French beans, peas, runner beans (legumes)

Lamiaceae/Labiatae: basil, Chinese artichoke, marjoram, mint, rosemary, sage, savory, thyme

Liliaceae: asparagus, chives, garlic, leek, onion, salad onion, shallot (alliums)

Malvaceae: okra

Poaceae/Graminae: sweetcorn

Polygonaceae: rhubarb, sorrel

Portulacaceae: summer purslane

Rosaceae: salad burnet

Solanaceae: aubergine, capsicum (sweet pepper and chilli), physalis, potato, tomato (solanums)

Valerianaceae: corn salad

Diversity on a small scale

If you have only one small bed, it is bound to have mixed plant families at different stages of a season. A healthy variety of different plants from many families is a good way of achieving some balance of pests and predators, and lowers the risk of suffering damage from any one disease.

summer beans, after spreading an inch or so (2-3cm) of compost or manure.

Sowing should be two or three weeks later than usual, so that plants do not outgrow the containers in August and early September. For example, kale and savoy cabbage could be sown in early July in modules, planted in 20-25cm (8-10") pots after three weeks, and watered regularly until planting. Some vegetables, such as Brussels sprouts and cauliflower, grow too large for this to be viable. Smaller varieties of kale are worthwhile.

Container salads

The vegetables I recommend for containers in winter are mostly salads, with a few carefully chosen vegetables.

- Land cress, endive, mustard and spinach all survive outside and make new leaves in mild winters.
- Herbs such as chervil, parsley and coriander are suitable for outdoor growing but will yield better indoors in midwinter.
- Container salads indoors, which can include lettuce and pak choi as well as those listed above, are probably the most worthwhile vegetable to grow in containers – see pages 196-8.

Container vegetables

- 'Red Russian' kale is well adapted to containers, being more compact than other varieties, and it has pretty leaves.
- Salad onions are compact and can be sown as late as September, or planted in October after summer crops have finished; they won't be ready until April – right in the middle of the hungry gap when you will bless every one.
- Garlic can be planted in containers to grow through winter while, for example, winter salads are cropping. After winter salad plants flower in early May, the garlic can finish growing strongly, having spent much of the winter putting down some strong roots.

Mustards planted in October in the greenhouse and picked through winter; this photo was taken before picking on 3 April.

Leeks could also be grown in this way, from a sowing in May. Whichever vegetable you choose, be sure to grow a true winter variety – such as 'Bandit' for leeks and 'Endeavour' for savoy cabbage, which mature in March and April – so that they have time to settle into their soil in autumn before growing again through winter. For kale I would choose a small variety such as 'Dwarf Green Curled'.

At the end of winter it is a good idea to top-dress containers with a layer of well-rotted manure or compost, right up to the top, to replenish their nutrient status and rooting area. Or you can empty containers on to beds and borders, then fill them with new multi-purpose compost.

Growing in shaded gardens

Vegetables like plenty of light to grow, but shaded plots can still be reasonably productive. Trees and hedges take a lot of moisture as well as light, but at least this aspect is less of a problem in winter, with more growth happening under deciduous trees in winter and spring than in summer. However, if there was an evergreen tree close to my vegetable plot I would surely bring out the saw, and plant a rose instead.

Herbs for winter

Many herbs are encouragingly winter hardy and one or two offer a surprising amount of new growth in any milder spells. Three that stand out are parsley, coriander and chervil, all members of the umbellifer family.

Perennials such as sage, rosemary and thyme keep some leaves in usable condition, but must not be over-picked. In late winter there is a reassuring burst of growth from established clumps of chives and sorrel, which become trusty friends during the hungry gap.

How to grow and harvest these herbs is explained in Chapter 8 (pages 121-3) and Chapters 10 and 11, and also in Chapter 15, because it is really worthwhile to have some biennial herbs under cover – to make more of their ability to grow for many months in low levels of light, even when being regularly frozen.

Chervil in late October after a frost of -6°C (21°F). It was sown late July and planted mid-August.

The same chervil after thawing, showing how leaves can recover well from occasional frosts.

Chapter 6

Tips for sowing & planting

Seeds or plants – a world of difference

Seeds and plants are the most important annual purchases you will make: success or otherwise depends on fresh, high-quality seed of suitable varieties and well-grown plants.

Seed can be sown either directly in the soil, or in compost indoors for later setting out as plants. There are good reasons for doing both and they are explained below.

Many winter vegetables are sown in late spring and summer, all at different times, so it's a good idea to write their sowing dates on a calendar to prompt you.

Sowing under cover is a really reliable way of getting young plants going, even in summer. See the table at the end of this chapter (page 77) for indoor sowing dates.

A look at seed

Seed is our starting point – its quality can affect everything else. To be sure of fresh seed, you can try saving your own. However, most of us use bought seed. Here I offer a few tips on seed you can buy, before giving advice on seed saving and sowing.

- **Freshness.** Seed is not always of the most recent season, and for certain vegetables this matters. I find that parsnip seed, above all, needs to be as young as possible, so don't hang on to any leftovers. Onion and leek seeds also grow best when fresh, but seeds of other winter vegetables should stay viable for two or three years after purchase, kept as cool and dry as possible.
- **Quantity.** Some packets contain only a few seeds, usually those of F1 hybrids, which are expensive to produce. Sow these seeds in the most perfect conditions you can manage to be sure of their successful germination.
- **Variety.** It is sometimes hard to tell which variety is most suitable, and descriptions are often more glowing than the growing may be. Expensive F1s have mostly been bred for uniformity in commercial growing and may not always be suitable for small gardens. Once you find a variety that works well in your garden, stay with it.

Right: Peas growing under fleece and pushing it up as they grow (the fleece was lifted to take the picture).

- **Small print**. Some of the suggested sowing recommendations on seed packets, mainly regarding timing, are too broad. Choosing the best sowing time is important – be sure to check the timings given in this book.
- **Authenticity**. Be prepared for occasional surprises – I notice from time to time that seeds are wrongly labelled. For instance, I once sowed two packets of 'Musselburgh' leeks from different sources and they were completely different varieties. Another time, lettuce seeds from the same packet came up as two different varieties.

Late July in a polytunnel: an overwintered lettuce ('Mottistone') has been allowed to flower.

The Resources section of this book includes contact details of seed houses that I have found reliable and who carry an interesting range.

Saving seed

Quality of seed may be assured by saving your own, but it is a tricky thing to do in a reliable way.

This is partly because some vegetables cross-pollinate when flowering – for instance, parsnip may cross with hedgerow cow parsley and produce seed of a smaller, fanged root – and partly it is because of the time needed. Most winter roots, leeks and many other vegetables are biennial, so they need to grow for a year before flowering and setting seed the following year. Then you won't know how good your seed is until the third year!

The tips offered here give some guidance on a complex subject that requires a lot of background knowledge. I suggest looking at the website of the Real Seed Catalogue (see Resources) for some excellent tips, explained most clearly.

For winter vegetables, an easy seed to save is broad bean, by leaving a few pods to dry, then

'Seedy experiences'!

Here are two contrasting seed stories from my garden. 'Red Frills' mustard, allowed to flower outdoors but not really looked after (for example, I never watered it) had many aphids and the seed turned out poor with about 20-per-cent germination. Whereas 'Grenoble Red' lettuce, watered and allowed to flower in a polytunnel, made seed that germinated fast and grew wonderfully, for many harvests the following winter and spring.

Front: bought seed of 'Rougette de Montpelier' lettuce. Behind: my recently harvested seed of 'Grenoble Red'. Both were sown on the same day.

Sowing in dry soil

* Draw out a drill a little deeper than usual and then water into the drill so that moisture soaks well in. Sow the seed, cover over with dry soil and do not water again until seedlings are well established. Roots go down into moisture and leaves rise up through dust. By sowing in this way, with just a little moist soil near the seeds and dry soil on top, success is more likely because slugs will be less prevalent.

shelling them out. This does mean leaving a plant or two for an extra month so the seeds can fully mature, and they may be in the way of another sowing. Also, broad beans do cross-pollinate, so if there is a different variety nearby you may be raising a new variety.

Squash seed is easy to save – just dry some off when cutting open a squash to eat – but if the plant was grown close to different varieties, or to courgettes, it may have cross-pollinated and turned into seed of a less desirable vegetable. To be sure of keeping a variety true, you need to hand-pollinate newly opened female flowers with pollen from male flowers of the same plant.

Garlic and Jerusalem artichokes are good for replanting and will grow true. Potato tubers can also be kept and replanted the following spring, but this carries a small risk of viruses accumulating, which show as less vigorous and prematurely yellowing leaves.

Sowing direct in soil

For sowing small seeds, soil needs a crumbly texture and a tilth in *only the top inch* (2-3cm). Firm (not compacted) soil below is excellent for seedlings, whose roots can then wiggle into any crevices at the same time as being firmly held in place. They germinate in fine compost on the surface, then root steadily into undug soil below.

For the most part a light raking, just on the surface – not deep at all – helps smooth out any large lumps to a sufficient degree. Soil does not need to be perfectly fine and even, because sometimes that results in 'capping' of its surface and a crust forming, which prevents emergence of tiny shoots.

Drawing drills can be done with many tools, from a draw hoe to an upside-down rake to a small ridger. When sowing in beds you shouldn't need a string, because the bed edges can serve for lines. Sowing rows across beds is often the easiest way.

For small seeds, aim for a drill of about an inch (2-3cm) deep, and nearly twice that for larger seeds, such as beans, peas and sweetcorn, which may also be dibbed individually. Know the right spacings, as given for each vegetable in Part 3, and be especially careful not to sow small seeds too thickly. Turnips and carrots for example, when thickly sown, need a great deal of thinning if you want decent roots, as opposed to a large quantity of leaves.

Use a rake to draw soil back over the seeds and tamp the surface down with the rake's back. In dry weather you can walk on the drills to firm soil and retain moisture. If the soil is wet, tamp more lightly.

If deep mulches have been used that contain large amounts of undecomposed matter, such as straw, paper and grass mowings, I recommend using pre-raised plants rather than sowing seed direct. And after removing a polythene mulch, wait a week or so before sowing, so that slugs living under the mulch have moved away or been eaten by predators.

Preparing soil and sowing parsnips

1. Raking through compost on top of the soil to break up the biggest lumps.
2. Drawing drills in the surface compost, about 3cm (1") deep.
3. Sowing parsnip seed, with the hand close to the soil surface in case of wind.
4. Here the parsnip seeds are sitting on top of the soil, with compost at the drill's sides.
5. Raking over the top of the bed so the seed is covered with the compost.

Sowing large seeds

* Sowing individually is sometimes easier for large seeds, especially broad beans, which are happy to be buried 7cm (3") deep. Firstly, use a hoe to mark a shallow line of the row you want to sow, or use a string. Then dib individual holes for each seed, and finish by raking soil over the holes to refill them. I also use this method for garlic cloves, onion sets and potatoes, all at slightly different depths.

Planting into holes already dibbed – planting is quick once holes are made.

Starting with plants

The advice here is intended to guide you in growing or buying suitable plants, setting them out and protecting them where necessary.

Buying plants

The extra expense of buying plants is worthwhile for a small garden, where there may not be room to do your own propagation, and where only a few plants are needed. They may cost only a little more than a packet of seed.

When ordering plants, make a note in your diary of when they should come, although it's not always possible to know the exact day. If they are outdoor vegetables, unpack them as soon as possible, water them and leave them outside for a day or two before planting.

Planting

You can use various different tools for planting out. Dibbers are quick to use and make perfectly sized holes for small plants, when pushed in gently – or strongly in dry weather – and rotated a little. Make the hole a little deeper than the plant's rootball, then push the rootball or roots in firmly so that good contact is assured around all edges.

Planting tools

Dibber Small dibbers with a metal tip are commonly available, but longer dibbers are much easier to use. Make your own long dibber to save bending, get a clearer view of the planting pattern and enable deeper holes when needed. I buy a wooden spade or fork handle of 60-75cm length (2-2.5') and chisel some wood off the tapered end to make it more pointed, then sand the wood to make it smooth and apply some oil such as linseed to preserve the wood.

Trowel Use a trowel for larger plants. I like copper trowels because they do not rust, helping to keep a sharp edge and making it easier to insert them cleanly and create a nicely sized hole, especially in dry conditions. Avoid making holes that are too big, because soil structure is then lost and the larger area will need extra firming down after planting.

Bulb planters These make a hole of only one size and are difficult to insert in dry soil, but can work well for potatoes.

It is advisable to give a little water straight after planting, unless rain is imminent. Directing a small dose, either right on top of plants with a rose, or on the soil around plant roots with direct water, helps assure connection between soil and their compost. In warm, dry weather a second small dose of water for each plant is worthwhile a couple of days later, in case the existing rootball dries out before roots can organise themselves to tap into surrounding soil moisture.

Protecting plants

All fleece and mesh can be laid directly on top of small plants, just after they are set out. It wants to be quite tight, held down by a few stones or wooden poles along the sides. As the vegetables grow they push up the cover and an aerated, watered and mostly insect-free environment exists around their leaves.

For a bed width of 1.2m (4') I recommend a 2m (6')-wide roll of fleece or mesh, but 3m (10') or more for covering tall brassicas, such as broccoli and Brussels sprouts. Rolls of 50m (165') are cheaper to buy than shorter lengths, so finding somebody to share part of a long roll will save you money (see Resources).

Fleece

Fleece should do for many seasons' use if you buy the thicker grade, of 25 or 30 grams per square metre (gsm). Even when a little holed and torn, fleece creates a cosy environment. Don't worry about cutting pieces to the exact size of each planting, just roll up any spare fleece or mesh and tuck it underneath, with a weight on top. Then it will serve again on a larger area if need be.

Mesh

Mesh is more ventilating than fleece and is useful as summer protection for all brassicas, against caterpillars mainly, and for leeks against leek moth. Finer grades should keep out most flea beetles, aphids and midges. Both fleece and mesh will need removing periodically to weed.

Straight after planting out, and mainly from June until September, some winter vegetables will benefit from being covered with mesh. Throughout the summer, covers of white

Fleece for three seasons

Fleece is useful in spring for covering new plantings such as celeriac and squash, for two to four weeks. Then, before the nights turn too frosty in autumn, fleece can be laid over vegetables that do not like being frozen too hard, such as hearting Chinese cabbage. It can also be laid on winter salads in November, although in really severe winters it may not be enough. In the bitter December of 2010 fleece saved about half of my hearting chicory and all of the non-hearting, none of the hearting endive, and half of the red mizuna.

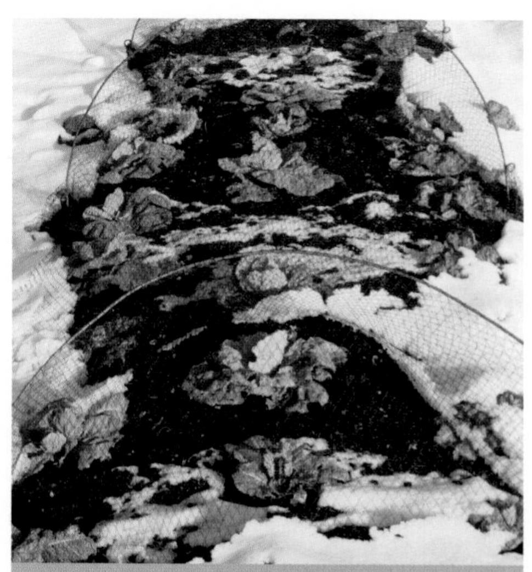

Spring cabbages in February, netted against pigeons; they gave welcome harvests in April.

mesh can protect brassicas from butterflies and thus prevent caterpillar damage. In addition they offer some relief to plants from smaller insects, and retain moisture in hot, dry weather. Also, they can keep root flies out of a carrot bed if in place by early August. Leek moth, a relatively new pest in Britain, can be kept out of leek beds if mesh is applied straight after planting leeks in midsummer and kept in place, apart from weeding, until about the middle of September.

Netting

Where pigeons or other birds are suspected, an alternative to fleece or mesh is lightweight netting with holes of any size from 1cm to 5cm (½-2"). I use netting with 2.5cm (1") holes, 4m (13') wide and with a life expectancy of ten years. Suspend it above plants, for example over cloche hoops, or hold it up on wooden posts with upside-down pots on top for the netting to nestle on. A few stones along the net edge will be enough to keep it in place. Bird damage is a risk with all brassicas, spinach, beetroot seedlings, chard and sometimes salads.

Propagation in trays, modules & containers – indoors or out

Plants can be raised outdoors between April and September. This section also looks at sowing seeds under cover in an environment where temperature and moisture are controlled

Red komatsuna and 'Red Frills' mustard in October, sown a month earlier and now ready to plant out.

Raising your plants

* Support plants using wooden, slatted and raised staging, such as old pallets with wooden legs. Air at waist height is warmer and drier than at ground level, and there are fewer slugs.

enough to ensure reliably successful growth of tender seedlings and young plants. See the table on page 77 for recommended indoor sowing and planting times.

Here are some really worthwhile benefits of sowing seeds in trays, modules and containers, for planting out later:

- Better germination, making the most of expensive seed.
- Less damage to seedlings by slugs and insects (especially indoors).
- More success with second cropping through time saved by planting rather than sowing.
- More even spacing of vegetables, with fewer gaps.

Containers for sowing

Many kinds of containers may be used, as long as there are drainage holes at the bottom so you can water without danger of saturation.

- **Trays** Smaller seeds can be sown into any undivided seed trays, module trays or home-made trays such as old egg boxes.
- **Pots** Most pots are now made of plastic and this is fine, as long as there is a hole in the bottom. Pots are suitable for larger seeds only, and should be watered sparingly until plants are growing strongly.
- **Modules** Trays that are divided into compartments, called modules, cells or plugs, enable small plants to grow in their own mini pot of compost and then be planted out or potted on without root disturbance. They are usually made of plastic, sometimes thin and flimsy, so look for the sturdiest ones you can find, with 24-60 compartments per tray of about A4 size.
- **Lengths of smooth guttering** These are another option, filled with compost and sown as for a row in the soil outside. Lay them slightly sloping on the staging so water can drain; seedlings can be thinned as necessary. At planting time, make a long hollow in the soil, slightly deeper than the gutter, then slide the whole contents of the gutter into it. It sounds like an easy way of instant gardening but actually takes practice to do well – having the compost fully moist is a help in sliding it out.

Container size

* The best size of container is related mainly to the size of seed: larger peas and beans are better in pots and large modules, while small-seeded lettuce, salads and cabbage do better in seed trays and small modules. Avoid sowing small seed in large pots, because unnecessary space and compost are required, and it is too easy to over-water.

Compost for sowing

Seedlings and plants need to grow vigorously in a small rootball of compost that is free-draining and full of nutrients. Therefore, when sowing into containers of any kind, it is worth spending time making, or money buying, some special compost. Do not use garden soil because it has insufficient nutrients and drains too slowly.

Some commercial composts are for sowing ('seed compost') and some are for growing ('multipurpose compost'). In practice I find that the latter serves for almost everything and is possible to use at all stages of growth, except for lettuce and basil, which germinate better in free-draining seed compost.

Home-made compost can be used for potting when it is of good quality and has been sieved, which is easiest if the compost is not too wet, otherwise it makes a ball of sludge in the sieve. Then add and mix nutrients such as seaweed meal, chicken pellets, wood ash (some of any, or a little of all, as per handfuls below) and also some sharp sand or vermiculite for holding air. Use about three or four handfuls of nutrients and eight or ten of sand or vermiculite per bucket of compost.

Watering

Seed composts have fewer nutrients and more particles for drainage, which keeps the tiny roots and leaves drier, emphasising how you need to be careful when watering seeds and seedlings – they need little water and may die of mildew if watered too regularly in seed trays. The mildew is called 'damping off', when leaves suddenly wilt as if they are too dry, whereas they are in fact too wet.

Observe closely while watering, regarding how much to give – is the compost cracking away from edges or is it dark and damp already? – and watching for any potential issues such as damping off, attacks by pests, and plants becoming ready for planting or potting on. Watering of modules and pots is a daily necessity in sunny weather and for larger plants, but is needed only every two to three days in damp weather and for small plants.

Pricking out

When small seeds are sown in seed trays, and have reached the stage of two or three leaves, they can be 'pricked out', which means transplanting them into modules or small pots. All vegetables except carrots and parsnips can be

Pricking out seedlings

1. Lettuce seed was sown into a seed tray and now, five days later, the tiny seedlings are being lifted out with a pencil.
2. I separate the seedlings and push them into pencil-sized holes, burying the stems to make sturdier plants.
3. Three to four weeks later, plants of 'Grenoble Red' lettuce are ready to go out.

treated in this way and it is much easier to sow celeriac, for instance, in a small tray and then prick out the seedlings than to apportion its tiny seeds between modules.

You need only a pencil to do this delicate operation and it is easier than it may seem initially, when you observe these guidelines:

1. Plants to prick out should be handled by a leaf rather than by stems, which may otherwise be terminally crushed.
2. Use a pencil, inserted underneath their roots, to lift out seedlings from below.
3. Make a pencil-sized hole in a pot or module and push all the root of one plant into it; also most of the stem, if seedlings have drawn up to the light, to keep seedlings compact and sturdy.
4. Gently firm compost around the seedling's roots and stem with pencil and finger.
5. Water the pricked-out seedlings with a fine rose.

Potting on

When starting to outgrow their small pot or module, tender plants such as celeriac and squash can have their rootball tapped out and gently buried in a larger pot of compost, usually with a bit of stem covered by the compost as well, to keep them sturdy. Spread the new pots out a little, to allow light from all sides.

Planting out

Plants with leaf colour turning pale are a sign of nutrient depletion. They can either be potted on or, if you feel they are large enough and the season is right (see advice for each vegetable in Part 3), they can be moved outside to a bench or small pallet, just off the ground, for one to four days before planting in their final position.

Planting size varies with each vegetable and the size of tray, module or pot. Larger plants tend to resist pests better but take more time to recover from 'planting shock' as they adjust to life in the soil outside.

Mizuna in a larger module has grown larger than winter purslane in a smaller module.

Be prepared for the 'paralysis' that comes over plants after they have been set in their final destination. For a week or ten days they look hesitant, and while in this frame of mind they are vulnerable to slugs. Then suddenly they green up and look stronger, and a tricky stage of growing is successfully achieved.

Pest problems with indoor propagation

* Keep a look out for slugs – they can make whole seedlings disappear, or take bites from leaves. If this happens, check for them under pots or any other objects offering hiding places in the propagating area. You can also look for slugs at night with a torch and a sharp knife.

Mice like seeds of lettuce, beans, etc., so it is worth having traps primed from August until October, when mice are coming indoors and the time for sowings in the new year is approaching.

Indoor sowing for outdoor winter vegetables *(Only those which can be and are worthwhile sowing indoors)*				
Vegetable	**Recommended sowing dates**	**Heat?**	**Pot on?**	**Plant out**
Asparagus	Feb–Mar		Yes	June–July or the following Mar
Beans for drying	May	Optional		May–June
Beetroot	June			July
Broccoli, purple sprouting	Early June			June–July
Brussels sprouts	May			June
Cabbage, spring	Late Aug			Late Sept
Cabbage, winter (ballhead)	May			June
Cabbage, winter (savoy)	June			July
Cauliflower, spring	June–July			July–Aug
Celeriac	Mar–early Apr	Yes	Optional	May–June
Chard / leaf beet	July–early Aug			Aug
Chervil	July–early Aug			Aug
Chicory (forcing)	May–early June			May–June
Chicory (heart)	July			Aug
Chicory (leaf)	Late July–early Aug			Aug–Sept
Chinese cabbage	July–early Aug			Aug
Coriander	July–Aug			Aug
Corn salad (lamb's lettuce)	Late Aug–Sept			Sept–Oct
Endive (heart)	Early Aug			Aug
Endive (leaf)	Mid–late Aug			Sept
Kale	June–July			July–Aug
Land cress	Aug			Late Aug–Sept
Leek	Apr			May–June
Lettuce	Late Aug			Sept
Onion, bulb / shallot	Jan–Mar	Optional		Mid-Mar–late Apr
Onion, salad	Late Aug–early Sept			Sept
Oriental leaves	Aug–early Sept			Aug–Sept
Parsley	July–early Aug			Aug
Peas for shoots	Feb–Mar	Optional		Mar–Apr
Rocket, salad	Late Aug–early Sept			Sept
Rocket, wild	Early Aug			Aug
Rhubarb	Mar–May		Yes	May–June or Nov–Dec
Seakale	Mar–Apr		Yes	May–June
Sorrel	Mar–early Aug			Apr–Sept
Spinach	Aug			Aug–Sept
Squash, winter	Apr–early May	Yes	Optional	May–early June
Swede	June			June–early July
Winter purslane	Late Aug			Sept

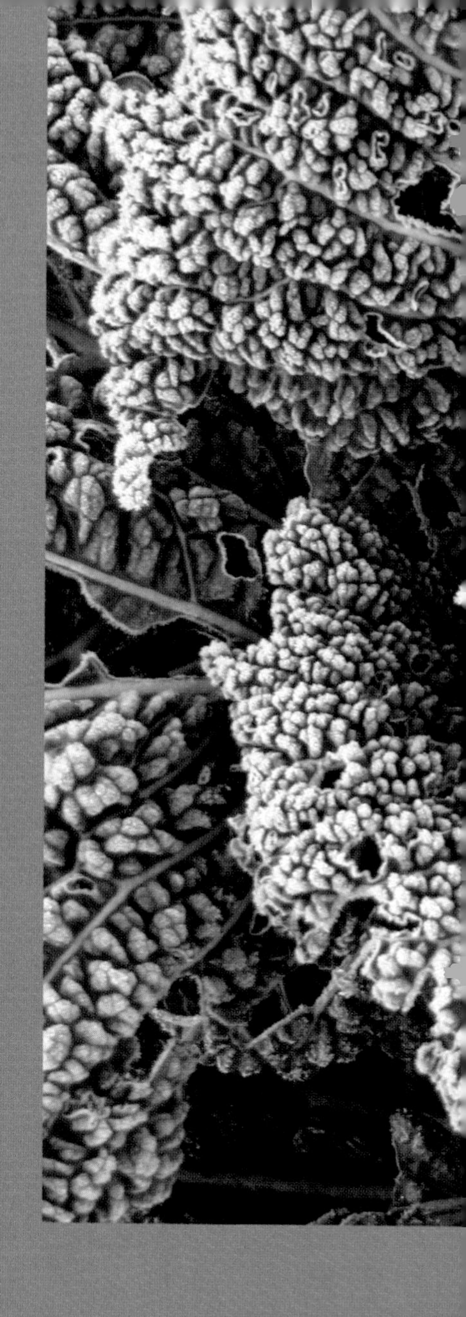

PART 3
Sowing, planting & growing calendar

Chapter 7

Sowing & planting in spring

Main-season vegetables – the staple foods of winter

This and the next two chapters offer advice on a wide range of vegetables that can be either harvested in winter or stored for winter use. All the sowings and plantings you can make in each month from March to September are explained: these starting times for winter harvests are well spread out, and I hope that having a chapter for each season helps you appreciate the long period in which you can sow and plant.

The advice given here is specifically for vegetables to harvest in winter, to store for winter and to overwinter as small plants for harvesting from April to June. Vegetables to sow in late winter, to grow rapidly and offer harvests in the hungry gap, are covered in Chapter 11.

A busy time

Late spring and summer is the main period of sowing for winter and needs careful attention, at a time of year when you are often busy with weeding, watering and gathering some plentiful harvests. I know from experience that the temptation in summer, with lots of produce to pick, is to feel that 'the granary is full', making it all too easy to forget some important sowings for winter harvests.

While many sowings are best made at a particular time, especially after midsummer when daylight is diminishing, in these chapters I generally also provide other possible dates that should still work, in case you miss the best week or two.

Keeping the plot undug and clean of weeds is a great help for summer sowings and plantings, because the soil is ready at any point, after clearing any debris from an earlier harvest. When you keep soil in good heart with enough organic matter, two harvests a year is certainly possible, and having the plot full at all times gives more incentive to stay involved, keep on top of weeds and admire the beauty of it all.

Right: Late April. These radish were sown at the same time as the rows of parsnips on either side.

MARCH

	Indoors	Outdoors
Sow	Asparagus, celeriac, onion, rhubarb, seakale	Parsnip, onion
Plant		Asparagus, Jerusalem artichoke, onion/shallot sets/bulbs & plants, potato, seakale
General	Pick increasing amounts of salad.	Weed all beds and growing areas. Knock out surface lumps of soil and compost.

March is often a cool month, but after mid-month there is enough warmth in the soil for some seeds to start germinating and for early growth of onion sets and tubers. Celeriac and perennial vegetables can be sown indoors.

Asparagus

- **Best sowing time: February to March indoors**
- **Best planting time: March, and crowns must be planted by the middle of April. Plants from seed grown in pots can be planted in summer**
- **Plants cost more than seed but save a year of waiting**
- **First harvests after two years are small but plants can live for 20 years**

Varieties

'Connovers Colossal' is an old favourite and reliable, but some of its stems bear berries, whose seeds can become a significant weed. F1 hybrids such as 'Jersey Knight' are increasingly available: they are all male so do not set seed, grow more numerous spears and are a little more vigorous. Their higher price should be offset by many years of good harvests.

Sowing

Sow by early spring, preferably indoors in small pots or modules.

Asparagus grows readily and has no special requirements, though growth is faster indoors. After about two months in a module or pot the young plant can be potted on to a 7cm (3") pot.

Planting out

Young plants can be set out in midsummer if you are able to keep them watered in dry weather. Or, after a year's growing, your plants can go out in March – just make a hole with a trowel for the pot and its roots.

Plant crowns in March, in holes large enough to accept their spreading roots, about 10cm (4") deep. Soil for planting must be clear of all weeds, especially perennials: it is worth covering weedy soil for a whole year before planting asparagus.

Spacing

You may be tempted to crowd the plants a little, but in time they benefit from a lot of space so do plant them wide, at 60x75cm (2x2.5'). In clean soil you can grow other vegetables, such as salads and beetroot, between plants in their first year.

Subsequent growth

Two years' growth with no harvests taken allows plants to develop strong roots, which can then give a light harvest from late April and through May in the third year. By year four you can cut all spears that grow until the

New asparagus spears in early May. The roots of these plants are seven years old.

The same plants in August, after picking of spears was finished in late June.

third week in June, when plants should be left to grow tall and feed their roots again for the rest of the growing season.

Problems

Asparagus beetle is the main pest, and when prolific these beetles can eat a lot of stems and leaves, but I see them mostly on soil that is not mulched with good-quality organic matter.

Growing great asparagus

* Leave the fern-like stems to die down in autumn before clearing them and spreading some compost or manure. Keep the patch well weeded at all times, taking care to prevent any perennial weeds from establishing. There is no need to make trenches and ridges unless you want white spears – which is a lot of work for scant reward, as green asparagus is so delicious.

Celeriac

- **Best sowing time: the first half of March as long as some extra warmth is provided**
- **Other possible times: late March to early April**
- **Seed is best sown under glass or plastic, on the surface, and kept at around 20°C (68°F) for two weeks, then provided with some warmth on cold nights**

Celeriac prefers heavy soil and plentiful organic matter to make large roots – it has a lot of superficial roots and does best when they are supplied with regular moisture. Hence it grows best on clay soil – when I am asked by gardeners why their celeriac has grown so poorly, I nearly always find that the soil is light and free-draining.

Adding a lot of organic matter – as much as 7cm (3") on top – will help this, but on light

'Ibis' celeriac plants ready in May. They were sown mid-March in the greenhouse and pricked out in early April.

By October the celeriac has grown large, benefiting from a 5cm (2") mulch of cow manure on top of the soil.

soils you also need to water celeriac in any dry spells of weather if roots are to be large.

Varieties

Flavour-wise there is no great difference, but one variety stands out for the size of its roots: 'Prinz' has always outperformed other varieties in my gardens. Its leaves are compact as well, so it does not dominate other nearby vegetables, unlike, for example, 'Bianca del Veneto', which also gives miserably poor roots. Two other good varieties are 'Ibis', which initially grows faster than 'Prinz', and 'Monarch'.

Sowing

Celeriac needs a long season, so mid-March is a good general date, but this must be under cover as celeriac needs some warmth to germinate; also, if subjected to frost when small, plants may flower in late summer rather than swelling their roots. Later sowing until mid- or even late April is possible, but this will make the harvest smaller.

- Seed is best sown in a seed tray, for pricking out after about a month, because it is too small to sow individually in modules or pots. A windowsill serves well at this stage.
- Celeriac seed requires light to germinate, so leave it on the surface of moist compost.
- Covering with a clear plastic hood or a sheet of glass retains moisture and warmth. Once little green leaves are visible, seedlings can be pricked into modules.

Planting out

A good time to plant celeriac is mid-May to mid-June, with plants that are around 7cm (3") high. Water them well if the weather is dry, and give water every two or three days

Succeeding with celeriac

Weeds

* In the month or two of growing weather before planting, weeds germinate and can be hoed off when small. After planting, weeding should not be too tricky – be sure to hoe or hand-weed to keep on top of weeds at all times.

Water

* Hot summers are difficult for celeriac and sometimes they struggle to grow much. Give occasional water to keep them ticking over, then a spell of moist autumn weather can see them increase markedly in size, even through October.

after that if it stays dry, because celeriac suffers more than most vegetables from shortage of moisture, especially while establishing.

Spacing

Celeriac cannot make good-sized roots if planted too close; 30cm (12") is a minimum, and a 39-45cm (15-18") spacing is preferable to be sure that plants have enough room and moisture.

Problems

Lack of moisture and insufficiently fertile soil are the most common difficulties. Carrot root fly does tunnel in the roots but less so than in carrots and it is not worth protecting against.

Jerusalem artichoke

- **Best planting time: mid-March to mid-April**
- **Other possible times: until early May**
- **Easy to grow but they are tall plants that create shade**

Varieties

'Fuseau' has fewer knobbly bits; 'Gerard' has a red tinge to its skin. It is worth planting tubers that are as smooth as possible, but in years to come they may 'plant themselves' as volunteers from unharvested roots, which emerge in spring.

Planting

See above for dates – these are not too critical. Set tubers in 10-15cm (4-6") deep with a trowel.

Spacing

Planting 60cm (2') apart allows some good-sized tubers to develop.

Problems

There are few pests, although mice may enjoy some roots in winter. Jerusalem artichokes are one of the easiest vegetables to grow, but they are not suited to a small garden.

Remove re-growing tubers the following spring, unless you are happy to have another harvest from the same area. Or contain them by planting into a 25cm (10") pot buried in the soil.

Jerusalem artichoke flowers in October. Their close relationship to sunflowers is evident.

Onion (bulb) & shallot

- **Best sowing time: from January to March indoors; mid-March outdoors**
- **Seed is best sown indoors for good-sized bulbs**
- **Onions and shallots also grow from small bulbs called onion sets and shallot bulbs, best planted late March to mid-April**
- **Follow with autumn and winter salads and turnips**

Module-sown onions ready to plant, early April.

Varieties

There are many good varieties, for example, 'Sturon' is a reliable classic round onion, 'Stuttgart' has flat bulbs, 'Long Red Florence' has pretty pink, torpedo-shaped bulbs, while 'Hylander F1' and 'Santero F1' offer some resistance to downy mildew. Shallot varieties are also diverse and I suggest trying a few different ones to see which you like.

For red onions I have always been impressed by 'Red Baron', which shows less tendency to flower than other red varieties, especially when grown from seed, although it is susceptible to mildew.

Sowing

Both onions and shallots require a long season of growth, so mid-March is a final sowing date. Onion sets and shallot bulbs, on the other hand, should not be planted too early or they may flower in June and July; plant them from the equinox, 21 March, to mid- or even late April.

Seeds need covering with about 1cm (½") of compost and take about three weeks to emerge in a cold greenhouse. They grow happily together, with five or six seeds per module or small pot, not thinned but planted out and grown as a clump. This saves space and compost, for a harvest of many medium-sized bulbs rather than a few large ones.

Alternatively, they can be sown outside in drills about 2cm (1") deep, seeds 1cm apart – in weed-free soil, otherwise the slow-growing and fine-leaved seedlings may be quickly covered by weeds.

Planting out

Hunger for nutrients often causes module-grown plants to yellow at their tips when still small. They can either be potted on or planted out from about mid-March to late April; early April is the ideal time.

Sets and bulbs can be planted using a dibber to make holes about twice their length, so their tops are covered with soil. Birds may enjoy pulling them up for worms underneath, in which case a net should be laid for a month or so, weighed down with stones at the edges.

Spacing

Crowding is rarely a problem but closer planting results in smaller mature bulbs. For medium bulbs, allow about 10cm (4") all around or plant in rows of 30x5cm (12x2"). Multi-sown modules need more room, say 30x30cm (12x12") if there are four plants in each one.

Problems

Fungal attack is the main issue. White rot is a soil-borne fungus that persists for many years

The clumps of seedlings were planted without thinning, and are now ready to harvest in early August.

and kills plants quickly with snow-white mould around their roots; infected plants are best burned or binned. Luckily white rot is quite rare, but once established in soil it can last for many years. I find that not digging, with compost on top, has tended to diminish it.

Weed-free onions & shallots

✱ The leaves of these plants give minimal shade, so weeds can easily grow underneath them. Be prepared to hoe at first and then to hand-weed when they are larger, because the horizontal leaves of onions and shallots when they are well grown make hoeing impossible.

Onion downy mildew, also known as neck rot *(Peronospora destructa)* has become more common in recent years and appears as grey mould from about late May, taking just two or three weeks to turn leaves yellow. Small bulbs may have formed by then and can still be used but will probably not keep for long, rotting from the neck down. One remedy is to stop growing overwintering bulb onions, which harbour this mildew (and also suffer from it, but only when nearly full-grown), and, if you have an allotment, ask other allotment holders to do the same. You can also try a resistant onion variety, such as 'Santero F1'. Onions and shallots grown from seed are less likely to suffer than those grown from sets and bulbs, which are increasingly a source of mildew infection.

Parsnip

- **Best sowing time: March**
- **Other possible times: November to February, the whole of April and the first half of May**
- **Seed is best sown directly into soil; may also be sown indoors**
- **Parsnips grow well in most soils, including soil that has not been dug**

Varieties

I have grown many parsnip varieties and would grow all of them again. In 2009 I did a trial with seven varieties sown on the same day and they all performed well, also with little variation in flavour. By winter's end a few more differences were apparent, such as 'White Gem' being susceptible to canker (see page 89) and having a rather harder core than 'Tender and True' or 'White Spear', but its yield was still excellent, with broad shoulders.

There is an increasing number of hybrid F1 varieties, which offer a little more uniformity; useful if you want parsnips for the show bench.

Rows of parsnips emerging through compost in May, from a sowing nine weeks earlier. Radishes sown with them have already been harvested.

Sowing

Parsnip seed takes a long time to germinate and needs to be consistently damp for the whole time – as long as three weeks. This is one reason for sowing so early, because the soil is more likely to be damp in winter and early spring than in May and June, when a hot, dry week after seeds have started to germinate but before their roots have reached into moist soil below may frazzle them.

The other reason for sowing early is that parsnips then have more time to grow bigger. So if you want baby parsnips, they can be sown as late as early July – so long as the soil can be kept moist while they are germinating. Parsnip sowing is pictured on page 70.

- Drills can be deeper than for carrots, at least 3cm (1") and a little deeper in light soils.
- In undug soil the seed can be sown into compost on top, so it is then lying on the previous soil surface. Or it can be sown into soil with no added compost, then the emerging rows can be mulched with compost or manure in early summer.

The oft-quoted advice that soil for parsnips should not be manured or composted is associated with digging and the incorporation of organic matter, which encourages roots to fork. Organic matter on the surface is simply feeding the soil and encouraging healthier growth, without confusing plant roots.

Inter- & mixed sowing

Slowly germinating parsnip seedlings can be more easily identified when a few radish seeds are sown in their drills at the same time, at about 5cm (2") intervals. They emerge quickly and help to identify the parsnip rows, and are ready to eat before their slower-growing companions need much room. In clean soils, a row of radish can be sown *between* the rows of parsnips and harvested in May, well before the parsnip rows close over.

Parsnip seed is light and flaky, so it can be blown away on a windy day: your sowing hand needs to be held close to soil level as the seed is dribbled out of it and into the drill. In a dry March, when soil may already be a little dusty on top, I suggest firming the rows, once sown and filled back in, by walking on them. If growing parsnips indoors for planting out, options for sowing containers include toilet roll centres or root-trainers – these are suitably long and can be filled with seed compost: wet it well and sow with two or three seeds in each. Thin to the strongest seedling and plant out when the first true leaf is visible. Any delay, beyond the first true leaf, usually results in a round or forked parsnip.

Spacing

Rows can be across or along beds, about 45cm (18") apart, with seeds every centimetre at least and seedlings eventually thinned to 5-10cm (2-4") apart. The final spacing, which determines whether you will harvest large or small roots, depends on germination as well as thinning.

Weeding

Seed quality is often blamed for poor germination but other problems also contribute, such as the slowness of germination leading to seeds being lost under weeds.

Weeds are always an issue because so many of them germinate a lot faster than the parsnips. It may be that after three or four weeks all you see is a general carpet of green seedlings. Look carefully and the parsnip rows should be there, but it is quite a job to weed carefully in this situation, and it is essential that you weed before the emerging parsnip seedlings are smothered.

Sow parsnips in the cleanest soil you have, or spread a 5cm (2") layer of weed-free compost, such as green waste compost or spent mushroom compost, before planting. Also, I find that not digging leads to many fewer annual weeds, and after a year of keeping the soil clean, without any cultivations, it becomes mostly clean of weed seeds at the surface level, making it much easier to grow parsnips.

By late June or July, parsnip plants should be large enough to completely shade the soil below. At this stage it may be tempting to forget about weeding, but I urge you to continue looking for and pulling any weeds, before they set seed and cause problems for next year's sowings and plantings. You can also mulch between rows with compost in early summer.

Problems

Canker, a fungal infection developing around roots' shoulders in wet winter weather, is the main disease. Mostly it can be cut out before cooking. Varieties such as 'Tender and True' or 'Gladiator F1' have some resistance.

Carrot root fly is the principal pest and its maggots tunnel around the surface of parsnips. It is less annoying than on carrots because the extra size of parsnip roots mean the affected edges can be trimmed off.

Potato

- **Best planting time: March to mid-April**
- **Other possible times: until early May**
- **Tubers can be chitted indoors but this is not vital**
- **Potatoes like soft, crumbly soil or compost to swell their tubers**

Varieties

For winter eating, second early and maincrop varieties are best because they will sprout less in storage. Choose a variety according to which colour you want and whether you like floury or waxy, small or large potatoes.

'Charlotte' is a reliable, large, waxy second early, 'Bintje' and 'Remarka' are excellent-tasting maincrops and the 'Sarpo' range has the best resistance to blight, although its flavour and texture are not universally liked. 'Pink Fir Apple' is a reliable salad variety.

You can save your own seed and plant a few medium-sized tubers of last year's harvest, but doing this for more than a year or two may result in less healthy plants.

Planting

As long as they do not freeze, tubers sit happily in cool soil and grow slowly from about the middle of March. Planting in April is fine, but yield will suffer if you plant in May.

If space can be found indoors, it is worth buying potatoes in February to stand on end, so they grow sturdy green 'chits' or shoots which, after planting, more quickly become stems. Unchitted potatoes, or ones with longer, white shoots, will also grow successfully.

You can either draw out a drill of 7-10cm (3-4") depth or dib individual holes for each potato. In undug soil I plant tubers just below soil level, then place a ridge of compost or manure along the row.

Potato plants emerging in May through compost, cardboard and straw, which was laid on top of undug grass and weeds in January.

By late July there was a reasonable harvest, although some damage by slugs: these tubers of 'Harlequin' are growing in surface compost.

Signs of maturity

Potatoes grow fast and abundantly, so watering is beneficial in dry conditions and on dry soil. Then, after about four months, and assuming no blight has arrived, some yellowing of leaves indicates the end of the plants' life: for second earlies this happens in August; for maincrops in September; for 'Sarpo' potatoes, hardly at all, but a September harvest gives tubers of better flavour and with less slug damage.

Potatoes can be grown in sacks and large bags, but you will need extra time to look after them – watering and adding more compost – possibly out of proportion to the harvest. You may also need to empty out most of the compost from the bags to find the harvest.

Spacing

Second early and maincrop potatoes do best at a spacing of 45cm (18") in all directions.

Earthing up

If a late frost is forecast, earth or compost can be pulled from each side of a row to cover all growth (this is called 'earthing up'). Leaves then reappear and grow, before another covering of earth is pulled up after about a month, around the lengthening stems, to support them and, more importantly, to ensure that all developing tubers are kept in the dark – otherwise they turn green and inedible.

In undug soil, compost can be used to earth up, and more compost or manure can be added if you have enough. After the harvest of potatoes this leaves a beautifully fertile bed!

Problems

Blight is always the disease to be wary of, and it arrives after any warm, wet week from about the middle of June. The first indications are occasional brown leaves, and if it stays wet, plants can die FAST – within a week – by which time many tubers may already be infected. So cut stems off at the first sign of blight infection on plants. See Chapter 11 (pages 166-7), Chapter 12 and Chapter 13 (page 184) for more about blight and storing potatoes healthily.

Scabs on tubers are most common in alkaline soils, but they are cosmetic only.

Slugs like potato tubers, but damage is not too severe in drier seasons, on lighter soils and when tubers are harvested as soon as the foliage starts to die back.

Rhubarb

- **Best sowing time: March to May in small pots**
- **Best planting time: May to June as young plants, or November to December as roots**
- **Planting works well with any good-sized piece of root from an established plant**
- **Growth is faster from a root than from seed**
- **Best to wait a year after planting – harvest in the second spring**

Varieties

'Timperley Early' is best for stems in late winter and early spring.

Sowing & planting out

Sow by early spring, preferably indoors in small pots or modules.

Rhubarb from seed grows vigorously: it needs potting on after two months and can be planted out before midsummer.

You can set out home-sown plants after a few months, or after a year's growing in a larger pot. November is a good month to plant pieces

'Timperley Early' rhubarb in late January: this variety is consistently early and tolerates frost.

of root, which may have been chopped off a neighbour's plant, for instance. Rhubarb goes dormant in late autumn, so moving plants in that season is best, before new growth happens – from January if it is mild enough.

Spacing

The plants are greedy for space, moisture and nutrients, so give them a metre (over 3') in all directions.

Harvesting

In the first year after planting take no more than a few stems, to allow establishment time for roots. In future years you can harvest all new growth from March to June. I find it best to stop at the end of June, so that July and August's leaves, which are of lower culinary quality, can feed the roots.

Forced rhubarb

Roots can be dug up in autumn and brought into a dark, frost-free space to grow sweet, pink stems, but this exhausts the roots. Covering plants *in situ* with forcing pots in February is another way of sweetening the harvest, but it is best to remove the pots by April so that plants can recover in full light. Forcing is optional – we really enjoy the rhubarb that grows naturally, which has excellent flavour.

Problems

Quality issues arise when soil is lacking moisture and organic matter, so a 5cm (2") mulch of compost or manure every autumn is a good way to maintain plants' health, with some watering in dry springs.

Seakale

- **Best sowing time: March–April indoors, April–June outdoors**
- **Best planting time: May–June as new plants, March–April as bought plants**
- **Slow to develop**
- **Likes free-draining soil and full sun**
- **Harvests in April are a great delicacy**

Varieties

'Lilywhite' is the most common variety.

Sowing & planting out

Sow in spring or, for quicker results, buy a year-old plant in spring.

Seakale seed is perhaps not always fresh and I have found it difficult to germinate. Once growing, it will need potting on after about two months.

This plant of seakale had a pot over it for two weeks in April when it was growing strongly.

Plant into clean soil with no perennial weeds, preferably in early spring.

Spacing

Seakale is a medium-sized perennial, needing about 60-75cm (2-2.5').

Subsequent growth

No harvests can be taken for two years after sowing or one year after planting, and just a few leaves in the year after that, without forcing. So three years after planting is the first main harvest: if leaves are eaten green they can be picked in April, and in May as well, until the beautifully scented flowers develop in late spring.

Problems

The main difficulty is the length of time it takes to grow a good-sized root that can make enough stems and leaves in the spring.

Forced seakale

This is optional and is easy to do – simply place a pot over plants when they are starting to grow – but it but takes energy from the slow-growing roots, so I would always leave some roots unforced, for forcing the following spring, in rotation.

Jobs for March

March is a quiet time in vegetable plots, so there are excellent opportunities to prepare soil for sowing and planting. A thorough weeding is the first requirement: most annual weeds, such as chickweed, bittercress, meadow grass, goosegrass and groundsel, should pull out quite easily, after loosening of the soil by winter frost. Perennial weeds such as dandelion and couch grass need a trowel to loosen their tap or spreading roots: pull out as much as you can and be prepared to remove more growth when it reappears, less vigorously, in two or three weeks' time.

The surface compost on undug ground can be run through with a manure fork or rake to knock out any larger clods and make a finer tilth. Sometimes I use a fork for hitting clods to break them, then flick any larger woody bits or fibrous lumps into the pathways.

This all helps you to be prepared for much busier times ahead.

Under cover you should have an increasing amount of salad leaves to pick. If there is space, set out some pea plants for shoots (see Chapter 15, page 216). See Chapter 11 for hungry gap vegetables to sow in March.

APRIL

	Indoors	Outdoors
Sow	Celeriac (early April), leek, rhubarb, seakale, winter squash	Brussels sprouts, leek, parsnip, seakale
Plant	Prick out celeriac	Asparagus, Jerusalem artichoke, onion/shallot sets/bulbs & plants, potato, seakale
General	Pick abundant salad leaves. Remove flowering plants.	Knock out surface lumps of compost and soil. First hoeing of weeds. Cover tender plantings.

April is a busy time for sowing and planting, much of it for summer harvests, but you can also be starting a whole range of vegetables for winter. Some, like Brussels sprouts, Jerusalem artichokes and potatoes, need plenty of room to grow and may have you wanting a larger plot.

Brussels sprouts

- **Best sowing time: mid- to late April outdoors, mid-May indoors**
- **Other possible times: until late May indoors**
- **An alternative is flower sprouts, with purple rosettes of small leaves**

Varieties

New varieties keep appearing but most are hybrids, bred for growers who want a single harvest. Older varieties worth a try are 'Bedford Fillbasket' and 'Noisette', but be prepared for some 'open' sprouts of irregular size; the flavour should compensate. Hybrids that are worth growing for a post-Christmas harvest include 'Wellington', 'Doric F1', 'Montgomery' and 'Trafalgar'; the latter is reckoned to be least bitter. Check the small print to see that a late harvest is possible, because many varieties button up early and have less resistance to frost.

Flower sprouts are still rather new to evaluate but are worth trying for their good flavour and ease of growing. The only variety so far is 'Petit Posy F1', a cross between curly kale and Brussels sprouts, with maroon-coloured main leaves and purple-tinged clusters or rosettes of leaves on its stems – for picking in the same way as buttons of sprouts, from December until March, with lovely harvests in February. Breeding work is continuing and needs to, because the 'Petit Posy' I grew had some kale plants among the sprouts, all from seed in the same packet. The flower sprouts were smaller than Brussels sprouts until January.

Sowing & planting out

April is the classic time to sow but May works well too, especially for late-cropping sprouts.

You may need only one drill across a bed of 1.2m (4'), with seeds every inch or so (2-3cm). Indoor sowing can be done in seed trays for pricking out, or with two seeds per module, thinned to the strongest after germination.

Plant out usually in June: set plants deep so that all of the stem is buried. Firm in well and water if dry.

Spacing

Sprouts need room to grow: 45x45cm (18x18") is a minimum and 60x60cm (24x24") is good.

'Noisette' Brussels sprouts planted in early June, in soil that was pasture nine months earlier.

By late August the plants are growing strongly and have enjoyed a wet summer.

The space between can be planted with lettuce, for hearts or leaves.

Problems

I find that pigeons prefer sprout leaves to cabbage, whereas butterflies lay eggs on cabbage rather than sprouts. Bird damage is usually worst in late spring, just after planting, and then again in winter.

Flea beetle can massacre seedlings from outdoor sowings in spring, so it is worth covering seedbeds with fleece and keeping it on for about a month. Plants survive dry summers but need rain in autumn.

Protecting sprout plants

* A bed of sprout plants can be covered with netting to keep pigeons at bay, or with mesh to protect against cabbage white butterflies, moths and aphids. Make sure the net and mesh are wide enough to stretch over the plants, which grow around a metre (3') or more high. For a 1.2m (4') bed you need a 3.5-4m (11-13') cover: either fold it along both edges at planting time then unfold it as the plants grow, or suspend it from hoops or stakes. See also the box on page 103.

Leek

- **Best sowing time: mid-April outdoors**
- **Other possible times: until the end of April**
- **Seed can be sown in different ways – thickly in drills outdoors, or 3-4 seeds per module indoors**
- **Leeks thrive when plenty of organic matter helps to conserve moisture in summer**
- **They can be planted after harvests of spinach and early salads, early potatoes and cabbage, overwintered broad beans**

Varieties

For early winter, 'Autumn Mammoth' grows large but has rather less frost resistance than 'Bandit',' Atlanta', 'Edison' and 'Musselburgh': just be sure that the small print says something like 'very hardy' or 'late leek'. Many varieties are early leeks, bred to grow fast, with long stems which turn mushy in frost.

Sowing

Avoid sowing earlier than the dates given above, because if young seedlings are exposed to too much frost and cold they risk being confused into thinking winter has happened, and then flower at some point in summer or autumn.

As with onions, sow seed about 2cm (1") deep in drills, or 1cm (½") deep in modules with four seeds in each; the first spiky leaves should appear within two to three weeks. In outdoor rows, seeds can be sown close together, three per 2-3cm (1") with 30-40cm (12-15") between rows if you sow more than one row.

Planting out

Modules with two to four leeks each can be planted out when as little as 5cm (2") high, usually in May. They cannot be set deep, so need earthing up later if you want blanched stems. Leeks from an outdoor seedbed can be lifted from early June until July, when stems are as thick as knitting needles or even pencils. Dib holes about 10cm (4") deep, and water in after planting to wash soil down around the roots. You can dib deeper holes to have whiter stems, but growth may be slower when roots are too deep.

Spacing

Spacing really depends on how large you like your leeks. An average spacing is 30x10cm

Young leek plants offer no competition to weeds, and these need weeding now!

'Bandit', an extremely hardy variety of leek, in late April, still growing strongly.

Care of your leeks

* When planting leeks in soil that has already grown an early harvest of vegetables, it may be worth spreading a thin layer of compost.
* Weed regularly and give water if soil becomes extremely dry.
* If you want blanched stems they can be earthed up in autumn, pulling soil or compost up from each side.

(12x4") for individual plants, or 30x30cm (12x12") for multi-sown modules, which produce a higher yield of slightly smaller leeks. When planting winter varieties such as 'Bandit' after mid-July, spacing can be closer to allow for harvesting smaller leeks in April.

Problems

Rust – a flaky orange crust on leaves – is common when leeks are short of moisture. Two remedies are to plant in soil with plenty of organic matter, preferably on top, and to water in dry conditions.

White rot is terminal for leeks if they become infected (see pages 86-7).

Leek moth is unfortunately becoming common in much of England: its voracious caterpillar eats the developing heart leaves, killing small plants and slowing growth of larger ones, with damage to the outer sheath of their stems. The first signs mostly appear in September, with strip-shaped holes in leaves, especially the tender young ones, where small grey caterpillars may be found. Infected plants can be cut to the top of their stems to remove the pest, then left to re-grow, but harvests will be small. Probably the best approach is to cover a whole bed of leeks with mesh as soon as they are planted, in June or July, and keep them covered until about the middle of September. Planting pencil-sized plants by late June, so that they are large by the time of the leek moth's main season, is another way of reducing the caterpillar's effect.

Onion sets/shallot bulbs & plants

Onion sets and shallot bulbs can be planted through April: early is best, before long, thin shoots have grown out of the unplanted sets or bulbs, and to give them more time to grow. Plants grown from seed should be ready to go out during April; although they can also be planted in May, this will cause them to mature later and it may be harder to dry the new-grown onions or shallots before storing.

Potato

Maincrop potatoes, for autumn harvest and winter storage, can be planted throughout April and even until early May. Any later and the final harvest will be smaller.

Squash, winter

- **Best sowing time: early to mid-April indoors**
- **Other possible times: late April to early May indoors**
- **Seed is best sown under cover, so that plants have enough time for fruit to ripen**
- **Squash plants like rich soil and need plenty of space**

Varieties

There is no huge difference in flavour so it makes sense to choose a variety that matures early, such as 'Red Kuri', 'Hokkaido Red' or 'Sunspot'. 'Crown Prince' grows larger fruit and rambles further, while 'Butternut' takes longer to ripen than other varieties.

Squash seed sown flat and then pushed into compost in a tray of 5cm (2") modules.

Dealing with the exuberance of squashes

* In July and August it is worth pinching out the ends of stems that start to invade and crowd out other plants. Or loop them round so they grow back towards their roots. Keep pulling any weeds you see under the squash leaves, before they seed.

Sowing

In the British climate squash needs every ounce of sun and warmth to develop ripe fruit that will keep well through the winter. Sowing indoors in the middle of April, with a little initial heat if possible, should mean that plants are a good size for setting out in late May or early June.

Lay seed flat and cover with 1-2cm (½-1") of compost, in modules or small pots. They need warmth to germinate, so if April is cold a little extra heat will be appreciated, perhaps by sowing on a windowsill. After about three weeks the seedlings may be ready to pot on; aim to keep them growing until they can be hardened off after mid-May, or as soon as all risk of frost has passed.

Planting out

Wait until mid-May at the earliest. Covering with fleece for a fortnight or two can help plants to establish if there are cold winds.

Spacing

As much as 60-90cm (2-3') is needed for plants to spread and develop plenty of leaves. A little closer is possible if some trellis can be provided for plants to climb up, where by late summer they will look pretty as developing fruit hang downwards.

Problems

Early cold is tricky and fleece helps a lot. Slugs enjoy ailing squash plants, so aim to have sturdy plants and avoid planting too early.

Mildew on leaves after August, which slows new growth, is a natural part of the ripening process, so if plants are still young and with healthy leaves in late summer, fruit may not have time to ripen and develop a hard skin, which is needed for successful storage. Hence the emphasis on early sowing.

Jobs for April

The first annual weeds will be germinating en masse by the month's end and it is usually worth doing some hoeing as soon as they are seen. A hoe is most useful when weeds are still seedlings, and hoeing soil to a shallow depth is a way of clearing ground of many hundreds of weeds in a short space of time. Thick carpets of weed seedlings, if allowed to establish, become a major job to remove and a serious impediment to later sowings and plantings.

Continuing from March, surface-composted soil can be knocked around a little more to make a fine tilth. If the surface dries I often

'Sunspot' squash growing beside a young apple tree. Trailing squashes are good vegetables to grow near trees as long as some water can be given in dry weather.

walk on beds at this time to smooth them; this also conserves their moisture. Undug soil has a much firmer structure than dug soil and can easily bear a person's weight, once any recent rain has drained through.

Many early sowings and plantings do better for covering with fleece or netting, against birds and/or inclement weather – see the recommendations for each vegetable.

Under cover you may have a veritable abundance of salad leaves, increasing all the time as April goes on, until some of the plants start to make flowering stems instead. Remove them when no more worthwhile leaves can be picked, then spread 5cm (2") of compost or manure to have soil ready for planting tomatoes, cucumber, basil, chillies and other summer vegetables in May.

MAY

	Indoors	Outdoors
Sow	Beans for drying, Brussels sprouts, chicory for forcing, kale, rhubarb, winter cabbage (all types)	Beans for drying, chicory for forcing, kale, parsnip, purple sprouting broccoli, seakale, winter cabbage (all types)
Plant	Summer vegetables	Beans for drying, celeriac, potato, rhubarb, seakale, winter squash
General	Pick more salad leaves and remove flowering plants, then spread compost.	Cover tender plantings with fleece or mesh. Thin parsnips. Hoe weeds again.

After all the work done to prepare soil and plants, with little to see for it, May is often the first month when strong growth of vegetables gives a feeling of reward and excitement about harvests to come. Weeds grow too, so it is a busy time.

Beans for drying

- **Best sowing time: mid-May indoors**
- **Other possible times: late May to early June outdoors**
- **Plants are frost sensitive so can't be sown too early**
- **A whole season is needed for beans to mature and dry *in situ***

Varieties

Almost any bean grown for pods can also be left unpicked, for the seeds to swell and ripen. Runner beans make large red beans, for example, edible when cooked. The best flavour I have discovered is from borlotta climbing French beans, of red and white colour, which also have attractive and edible pods.

Sowing & planting out

Sow from the middle of May, aiming to have 7-10cm (3-4")-high plants ready as soon as the last frost date has passed.

These borlotta beans were sown in late May, planted out in June and picked late September.

Sow two seeds per module, or two seeds per station outdoors in warm areas such as south-east Britain, after mid-May, and thin to the strongest plant.

Plant after the last frost date, by the end of May or in early June at the latest.

Spacing

Set plants 25-30cm (10-12") apart in wigwams or in rows, with canes or sticks for plants to climb.

Easy in fine weather

* Slugs may nibble young plants, especially if it is cool in late May and June, and plants may need help to start climbing their stick.
* Once they are growing strongly, there is little to do except weed and wait for harvest; in a dry summer, some water will help pods to swell.
* Harvest time is when a good half of the pods are dry and pale in colour, with leaves falling off the plants.

Problems

Insufficient heat is the most likely difficulty; if summer is cool and wet, there may not be time for plants to make seeds and for the seeds to dry properly. But they can still be harvested as moist, fat beans to shell out, and frozen rather than dried.

Broccoli, purple sprouting

- **Best sowing time: May outdoors, early June indoors**
- **Other possible times: from mid-April to late June**
- **When sown in June and planted in July, purple sprouting broccoli is a second crop and many vegetables can be grown before it, in the same way as for July-planted kale (see page 104)**

Varieties

Until recently the main choices were between *purple* and *white sprouting*, to crop *early* or *late*. Now there are also F1 varieties (some of them for summer and autumn harvests), but I recommend sticking with the open-pollinated ones for winter, because they tend to crop over a longer season.

This broccoli, planted in July, is now established and growing well in August.

Sowing & planting out

April is often quoted as a good month for sowing, but will result in huge plants that need more space. It is better to sow in May outdoors and early June indoors, for good-sized plants that can be grown as a second crop after salads, carrots and early peas.

Sow and plant out as for Brussels sprouts (see page 94).

Spacing

These are vigorous plants, so early plantings

Staking is not obligatory

* The long stems of broccoli make them susceptible to falling over. They actually grow well when stems are partly resting on the soil, so staking is not really necessary and they can be gently pushed in a new direction if fallen into a pathway.

need 60cm (2'); later plantings should be closer, at 45cm (18").

Problems

As for Brussels sprouts (see page 95). In mild winters purple sprouting broccoli can accumulate a lot of grey aphids, but these are not usually a problem. Severe frost, below about -12°C (10°F), can rot stems, so covering with mesh or even a net should save plants from most damage.

Cabbage, winter

- **Best sowing time (indoors or outdoors): May for red and white ballhead cabbage, early June for savoy cabbage**
- **Ballheads are for storing, savoys are for harvesting through winter**
- **Savoys sown in June and planted in July can follow salads, spinach and early peas**

Varieties

The hardiest winter cabbages are crinkly-leaved savoys such as 'Endeavour F1', 'Ormskirk Late', 'Tourmaline F1' and 'Rigoletto F1'. They can be sown a little later than smoother-leaved and more tightly hearting ballhead varieties such as 'Marner Large White', 'Marner Large Red' and 'Red Flare F1'. Two F1 varieties, 'Celtic' and 'Tundra', are crinkly-leaved ballheads that stand well in frost, as does 'January King'. There is a lovely sweet, pointed cabbage called 'Filderkraut' which makes large hearts when soil is fertile.

Sowing

Any time in May is good for ballhead cabbages; early May sowings tend to make larger hearts. Late May is better for savoys, while sowing savoys in early June results in small hearts by Christmas, after which they mostly continue to grow slowly and heart up until early April. Sow as for Brussels sprouts (see page 94).

These 'Filderkraut' cabbages were covered with mesh when planted eight weeks earlier on 1 July, but they grew too tall and butterflies were able to fly underneath the edges, so I removed the mesh.

Protecting against pests

* The extent of caterpillar and aphid damage to brassicas such as these cabbages lessens in wet summers and in windy gardens, because cabbage white butterflies and moths find it more difficult to fly around. So covering with mesh is not always necessary, depending on where you are and which brassicas are growing. The main heart of ballhead cabbages can be wiped out by tiny gall midges in summer, resulting in three or four small heads, so they are the most worth covering.
* Savoys for hearting in late winter are easier to grow because they have more time to grow away from any damage caused by insects in summer and autumn.

Planting out

Ballheads grow best in soil that has been bare until planting, but savoy cabbages may be planted as late as the middle of July, so there is time to grow some early salads or spinach before them.

Spacing

About 45cm (18") allows enough room for hearting. Closer spacing results in looser, smaller hearts.

Problems

These are the same as for Brussels sprouts (see page 95), but cabbages are easier to cover with mesh or netting because of their smaller height. Caterpillars can ruin hearts if they have time to burrow right in, so covering is unfortunately necessary for ballheads, whereas savoys can often survive without it.

Celeriac

Celeriac plants can be hardened off and then planted out any time after the middle of May. Earlier planting is unwise because, although they are not killed by frost, exposure of young plants to too much cold can make them flower in autumn, in which case the roots will be tough and useless.

Chicory (forcing)

- **Best sowing time: May**
- **Other possible times: June**
- **A winter salad, grown from roots that are dug up and forced indoors**
- **Plantings in July can follow early potatoes, salads, spring onions, carrots, etc.**

Varieties

The standard 'Witloof' is reliable and grows sturdy chicons (see Chapter 11, pages 160-1). I have tried F1 varieties such as 'Zoom' without noticing much improvement. 'Tardiva' grows lovely late chicons in March, which extends

A plant of 'Witloof' chicory in September, from a May sowing, with its root starting to swell.

Allow time for the harvest

✻ Chicory is easy to grow, although it can look a little ragged. Most time is needed at the season's end, for harvesting and potting up the roots – see Chapter 11, pages 160-1.

the season at a time when 'Witloof' is producing more stem than leaf.

Sowing & planting out

Sow any time in May, either indoors or outdoors, while sowing in June is also possible for slightly smaller roots. Sow a few extra seeds to allow for thinning a month later when seedlings are well established.

Sowing in modules works well, and results in forked roots, which is fine for forcing. Plants can be set out as late as July, allowing them to be preceded by many first harvests.

Spacing

Plants need room to make sturdy roots, 25x50cm (10x20") in rows or 40cm (16") each way. Growth is fast once established.

Problems

Tender chicory seedlings are appreciated by slugs, so take the usual precautions; raising plants indoors is helpful.

Kale

- **Best sowing time: May to early June**
- **Other possible times: until mid-July, for smaller plants**
- **Kale is easier to grow than cabbage and comes in many shapes and colours**
- **Kale planted in July can follow early potatoes, spinach, salads, carrots, etc.**

Varieties

There is a huge range of colours, leaf characteristics and plant height. 'Red Russian' has pretty, purple, flat leaves which also serve for salad, and it grows no more than 60cm (2') high. 'Cavolo Nero', also called 'Black Tuscany', has dark green, slightly crinkled, long, thin leaves on plants up to a metre (3') high but is less winter hardy; 'Pentland Brig' and 'Westland Winter' are of similar height and have large, curled leaves, while 'Dwarf Green Curled' has dark, curly leaves on a compact stem. The tall 'Redbor F1' is lovely to behold but slightly tough to eat.

Sowing & planting out

The sowing season is long, with May sowings, indoors or out, giving harvests from August. I sow indoors in early June for planting out in early July, after harvests of early salads, carrots, garlic or peas. July sowings will result in half-sized plants, which, nonetheless, offer welcome leaves in winter.

Sow and plant out in the same way as for Brussels sprouts (see page 94).

Spacing

45cm (18") allows room for a good-sized plant to develop, while later plantings can be closer – around 35cm (14").

Problems

As for Brussels sprouts (see page 95).

Harvesting ideas for kale

✻ Some of the lower leaves can be harvested from late summer and through autumn, but don't pick too hard if you want leaves in winter. Another valuable harvest from kale is broccoli-type shoots in spring – see Chapter 11, page 163.

'Westland Winter' kale and purple sprouting broccoli in July, planted after spinach.

By October, conditions for most brassicas are excellent, with more moisture and less heat.

Potato

Early May is the latest date for planting potatoes. Seed potatoes will have sprouted strongly by now and need to have been exposed to light so that their sprouts are compact and are not broken during planting. See page 90 for details.

Squash, winter

Winter squash plants should be kept indoors until all risk of frost has passed; late May is a good average time to plant them, or mid-May if you can cover them with fleece – unless it is unusually warm. Plants for setting out should be about 15-20cm (6-8") high with a couple of true leaves.

Jobs for May

When parsnips are 3-5cm (1-2") high they can be thinned to 5-10cm (2-4") apart. Their final spacing depends on how you like your parsnips, large or small. Large ones are less fiddly to harvest on cold winter days.

May is often the first month of really fast weed growth, so be prepared to hoe a couple of times, or to hand-weed reasonably regularly. A plot's green edges should be cut and trimmed to prevent invasion by grass and weeds.

Even by the end of May, your plot will still have some empty spaces. Don't worry – there are still many important sowings and plantings to do in summer.

Chapter 8

Sowing & planting in early summer

Keep sowing for winter during summer's abundance

June and July are key months for *planting* many winter vegetables, most of which should be set out by the middle of July. These months are also good for *sowing* many seeds of winter crops, such as swedes, carrots and kale in June, then winter salads such as radicchio, endive and Chinese cabbage in July.

Early June is the best time for sowing vegetables such as the humble swede, which grows most strongly and healthily in the year's second half. Savoy cabbage is another excellent example, often sown too early in May and tending to heart up by late autumn, whereas early June sowings make no attempt to heart up before winter, and often look unattractive in late summer, from damage caused by caterpillars eating their leaves. But they develop plenty of roots, are extremely hardy and use any milder spells in winter to develop their hearts, at a time when green leaves are scarce and no brassica insects are present. Just beware larger pests such as pigeons, although they are less interested in savoys than in other brassicas.

Successional sowing

Summer plantings can follow harvests of vegetables that were overwintered or sown in early spring. This second cropping allows you to make more use of space, and leads to a cleaner plot, rather than leaving weeds to grow after a first crop.

But growing two harvests in a year also asks more of the soil, and, unless enough compost was spread in the previous autumn or winter – so that some is still visible on top in summer – it is worth spreading about another 2cm (less than an inch) on the surface before planting.

Right: A late June planting of lettuce, to finish by September for plantings of salad under a winter cloche.

JUNE

	Indoors	Outdoors
Sow	Beetroot, chicory for forcing, kale, purple sprouting broccoli, spring cauliflower, swede, winter cabbage (savoy)	Beans for drying, beetroot, carrot, chicory for forcing, kale, seakale, spring cauliflower, swede, winter cabbage (savoy)
Plant		Beans for drying, Brussels sprouts, celeriac, chicory for forcing, kale, leek, purple sprouting broccoli (late in month), winter cabbage (all types), winter squash (early in month)
General		Net brassicas if pigeons are hungry. Thin parsnips. Keep weeding.

Waiting until June to sow many winter brassicas, such as kale, swedes and savoy cabbage, helps to spread the workload. Also, there is probably plenty of weeding and edging to do, and the first harvests of summer to gather, marking an end to the hungry gap.

Beans for drying

Plants of beans to dry want to be in place during the first week of June if possible. Any later and they are unlikely to have enough time for beans to dry on the plant in September.

Beetroot

- **Best sowing time: June; sow early in month if you want larger roots**
- **Other possible times: May for enormous roots; first week of July for smaller roots**
- **Seed is best sown indoors in modules**
- **Can follow salads, peas, spinach and carrots, especially when raised as plants indoors**

Varieties

Beetroot has a lot of variety to offer, in root shape, colour and flavour. 'White beetroot' is one of the sweetest, closely followed by yellow – for instance, 'Burpees Golden' and 'Golden Detroit'. If you like an extra-earthy flavour and hoops of red and white, try 'Barbietola di Chioggia'. Good red varieties for winter use are 'Sanguina' and the ever-reliable 'Boltardy'. All the aforementioned roots are round, while a long one of sweet flavour is 'Cheltenham Green Top', whose roots are sweeter and deeper, giving extra resistance to frost.

Late September: module-raised beetroot planted in June. Some larger roots have been harvested.

Modules of beetroot (right) and chard, sown four weeks earlier, for planting without thinning.

Sowing

Early June is best for large harvests; early July is the last chance for roots of reasonable size.

Beetroot grows well from being sown in modules or pots and then transplanted. A big advantage of doing this is the extra time gained for an earlier crop to finish. Sow three or four seeds in each module and then, about a fortnight later, thin seedlings to four per clump (some seeds grow more than one seedling). Each module can be planted *without further thinning* – its clump of plants will grow together, with their roots pushing one another apart as they swell (see photo on page 152).

Planting out

Clear all weeds and any surface remains of the previous crop, then dib holes 45cm (18") apart. This spacing is for clumps of four beetroot on average and should result in medium-sized roots. Plant closer if modules have fewer plants; a little wider if you want larger roots.

Spacing

If sowing seed direct, draw out drills about 45cm (18") apart and sow seeds every 2-3cm (1"), then thin seedlings to 5cm (2").

Problems

Beetroot is relatively trouble free, of insects at least, although slugs often make small holes in roots, especially in late autumn.

A fairly common disease is a fungal rot, which results in black spots on roots, and yellow varieties are especially susceptible. I know of no remedy and put infected roots in the compost heap.

Birds sometimes eat leaves of seedlings, and a fleece or mesh cover for the first month may be necessary.

Broccoli, purple sprouting, & kale

When planted in June, these have time to grow really large, compared with later plantings in July. As with Brussels sprouts (see below), they can be inter-planted with catch crops of quick-growing lettuce. Again, be ready to cover them with mesh or fleece.

Brussels sprouts

Any time in June is good for planting Brussels sprouts. Make a hole deep enough to bury most of the stem and firm plants in well.

Because sprouts are such a hungry vegetable I do not grow a preceding crop, but it can help them to grow better if a few lettuce are planted out between them. Some plants seem to feel a little lonely when spaced widely and grow more strongly when other plants are nearby. The lettuce can be cropped for leaves or grown for hearts, and will be finished before all the space is needed by the sprout plants.

Cabbage, winter

Ballhead cabbages want planting before mid-month so there is time for dense hearts to develop, whereas savoys can go out as late as July. Be prepared to cover plants with either netting against birds or mesh against insects – see boxes on pages 95 and 103. This is easier when all winter brassicas are planted together in one block.

Carrot

- **Best sowing time: mid-June**
- **Other possible times: from mid-May to early July**
- **Seed is best sown direct in the soil**
- **Carrots can follow spinach, spring leeks or radishes, or be inter-sown between garlic and salad onions**

Varieties

There is plenty of choice, with variations in shape, colour and flavour. An old and reliable favourite is 'Autumn King', which stores well and has long, pointed roots. 'Berlicum' and 'St Valery' are two equally tasty varieties for keeping through winter. 'Early Nantes' is a good choice for late sowings, even into the first half of July in milder areas – it grows fast and also keeps well in cold conditions.

Some varieties have been bred to resist carrot root fly, but I have found them to offer only slight resistance.

Sowing & planting out

Sowings in early June may be eaten as small plants by the last spring hatchings of carrot root fly, so mid-month is safer, and still gives time for good-sized roots to develop. Carrots mature to a good size within four months, sometimes in only three.

Outdoor sowing is easier at this time than in spring, when germination can be interrupted by cold weather. Sowing carrots in modules for transplanting is possible, but take care to plant them out when seedlings are still small, with no more than one true leaf, in case tap roots have reached the bottom of their pots, which leads to forked roots.

Spacing

Row spacings of any distance from 30cm to 45cm (12-18") are possible, according to how large you like your carrots. Sowing two or three seeds per centimetre (five or six per inch) should allow, after thinning, sufficient room for large roots to grow, about a centimetre (half inch) apart. Thinning is more important for having roots of a good size to store.

Problems

Carrot root fly is always a persistent pest, with the ability to make roots almost inedible when many maggots succeed in hatching: they tunnel around and through roots at different levels. There are a few flies around all summer, then their main season is late September and October. Dry summers keep them at bay, to a point, because the flies' eggs need

Inter-sowing

This works best in soil with few weeds and is a way of temporarily double-cropping a piece of ground to save time. Carrots grow slowly at first and need few nutrients at this stage; sowings in June can be made between any maturing crop that offers enough light and is not removing too much moisture. Garlic is the most suitable example because it is finishing its growth in June and is then harvested in early July.

Spring-sown salad onions can also be inter-sown with carrots.

Soil needs to have been well composted when the garlic or onions were planted, to have sufficient fertility for winter carrots as well. Rows 30-40cm (12-16") apart are ideal for sowing carrots between in June. Take care when harvesting the garlic or onions not to disturb the rows of carrot seedlings.

Carrots protected by fleece over the whole bed. They have been mulched with compost.

moisture to wash them down to root level after being laid on the surface. The most reliable way to prevent damage is to cover all carrot plants with mesh, by early August. Another remedy is to make a polythene 'wall' around a carrot bed, about 60cm (2') high. This stops the entry of any carrot root flies because they fly close to the ground.

Stay interested in weeds

* Keep removing any small weeds from August to October, even after the carrot foliage is large enough to shade all soil, to prevent any weeds from seeding. Out of sight is out of mind, but if a weed does set hundreds of seeds, you will regret it when dealing with all those weed seedlings.

Cauliflower, spring

- **Best sowing time: June, or July for smaller plants**
- **Sowing can be indoors or outside; few plants are needed**
- **Cauliflowers can be planted after garlic, salads, early carrots and spinach**
- **A slow, risky vegetable because winter hardiness is not guaranteed**

This 'Jerome' cauliflower, planted early July and now frozen in October, survived to make a curd in April.

Varieties

Cauliflower varieties for overwintering have specific times of curd development. 'Winter 3 Armado April' may be ready in March if the winter is mild; 'Aalsmeer' and 'Prestige' can harvest as late as May. Unless you live in an area of only slight winter frosts it is not possible to harvest cauliflower in January and February, because the curds, unlike most leaves, are damaged by moderate frost.

Sowing, planting out & spacing

Cauliflowers want to be larger than cabbages by the onset of winter, hence the earlier sowing dates than for spring cabbage (page 126). This also makes them a main-season crop, demanding of much space and time.

Sowing may be inside or outdoors. Be sparing with seed, because cauliflowers need a lot of space to grow, so you won't need many plants. When planting, bury their stems to make them sturdy. Space about 60cm (2') apart.

Problems

Slugs and pigeons may eat leaves, but insects are more likely to be difficult, because of growing through midsummer. Cauliflowers are best covered with mesh from the day of planting until early autumn.

Severe frost in winter may damage plants and make them look rather moth-eaten, but by March you should be seeing healthy growth as a prelude to later harvest.

Celeriac

Plants of celeriac want to be in place before about mid-June, so that worthwhile roots have time to grow. Water them in well and again every two or three days if it is dry, until they look well established.

Chicory (forcing)

There is no rush to plant this; mid-June is fine. Watch out for slugs in the fortnight after planting because they love young chicory, but larger plants suffer few if any pest problems.

Leek

Leek plants for winter can be planted any time in June, even into July. Be sure to water them in well, especially when planting after other vegetables that may have used a lot of soil moisture. Leek plants that are thicker than a pencil will take longer to establish than small plants, and will benefit from another couple of waterings at intervals of a few days.

Squash, winter

If not already in the ground, squashes want planting before mid-June to give them a good chance of having time to grow and time for the fruits to ripen in early autumn.

Swede

- **Best sowing time: early June**
- **Other possible times: until late June indoors**
- **Seed is best sown indoors; outdoor sowings suffer pest damage**
- **Can follow spinach, salads or peas, especially when set out as plants**

Varieties

I have tried many varieties over several years, for example, 'Helenor', 'Ruby' and 'Marian', and they all grow similarly well.

Sowing & planting out

Swedes can be sown in May but their tiny leaves are easily damaged at that time by flea beetles, which are most numerous in spring and can make enough small holes in young

'Helenor' swede, grown in the greenhouse; 18 days after sowing, it is now ready for planting.

brassica leaves to kill plants. By June there are fewer flea beetles around and sowings are more likely to succeed, but they will still benefit from covering with fleece, especially in dry weather.

Sowing indoors avoids many problems and deserves to be more widely practised, because module-raised seedlings transplant as easily as beetroot. Sow two or three seeds per module or small pot, then thin to the strongest as soon as possible – about ten days to a fortnight later. Plant out from late June to mid-July: you can plant in soil that you have already used for spring vegetables such as lettuce, spinach and early peas.

An underrated vegetable

Most difficulties in growing swedes arise from poor growth of seedlings: pay close attention to sowing dates and methods for reliable results. Swede is one of the more compact brassicas, an excellent winter vegetable and suitable for small spaces, especially when planted rather than sown. Swedes make a lot of growth in autumn, and roots continue swelling into November. Also they resist a huge amount of frost – see Chapter 11, page 169.

Spacing

30-40cm (12-15") is enough for medium-sized roots to develop, as long as soil is in good heart with compost or manure added, either in the preceding winter or spread as a mulch around growing swedes before the end of summer.

Problems

Being a brassica, swede leaves may be eaten by pigeons and caterpillars, if they survive the spring flea beetles. Fleece or fine mesh over sowings and plantings is worthwhile. In my garden I usually remove it in August, once plants are established, as long as pigeons are not around, because caterpillar damage to swedes is much less than to cabbages.

Cabbage root flies usually manage to lay some eggs around roots and you then find thin tunnels of damage, but they are close to the skin and easy to trim off before cooking.

Clubroot is more serious, and if you know this to be present, the best bet is a variety with some resistance, such as 'Invitation'. Wild animals such as deer enjoy swede in cold winters.

Jobs for June

If you have not already thinned your parsnips (see page 105), you can do so in June.

Weeding is ongoing and can be more time consuming in June than later in summer, because many vegetables have not yet grown enough to shade the soil.

By the end of June, there will probably be few empty spaces in the plot, with an abundance of plants growing and some that are ready to harvest, such as lettuce, spring onions, spinach, radish, beetroot, carrots, broad beans, peas and early potatoes. Then, once they are harvested, soil can be cleared, cleaned and planted with second crops – some sown in June, some still to sow in high summer.

JULY

	Indoors	Outdoors
Sow	**Early July:** chard / leaf beet, chicory for hearts, kale, parsley, spring cauliflower **Late July:** chard / leaf beet, chervil, chicory for leaf, Chinese cabbage, coriander, parsley, wild rocket (see August)	**Early July:** carrot, chard / leaf beet, chicory for hearts, parsley **Late July:** chervil, Chinese cabbage, coriander, wild rocket (see August)
Plant		Beetroot, kale, leek, purple sprouting broccoli, spring cauliflower, swede, winter cabbage (savoy)
General		Thin carrots and possibly swedes and beetroot. Water celeriac. Clear ground as harvests finish.

Be wary of the seductions of July – there are wonderful harvests to gather and savour, the garden is full, meals are adorned with fresh vegetables now and for weeks or months ahead. But how many months?

Vegetables that see their final harvest in July include overwintered plantings of garlic and broad beans, and most early plantings of lettuce, carrots, peas, broad beans, cabbage, cauliflower, calabrese, spring onions, early potatoes and spinach.

This frees up ground for the impressive number of vegetables that can be sown and planted in July – several of them for harvesting in winter months.

However, the weather in July can cause some difficulties. On the one hand it may be hot and dry, so that new sowings and plantings need careful watering, at least until plants are well established. On the other hand it may be relentlessly wet, in which case slugs will probably cause damage to small seedlings.

In either case it is often easier to work with plants than to sow direct. Tiny seedlings are quickly mown off by summer slugs, whose appetite seems more voracious than that of spring ones. And well-grown plants can establish quite quickly in hot, dry soil that has enough organic matter to hold moisture from a couple of well-timed waterings, with water applied only to the roots of the plants – once at planting time and then again two or three days later.

Order of weekly sowings in July

An approximate order of sowing in July, for winter harvests, is as follows.

- **First week:** carrot (though June better), cauliflower, chicory for hearts, kale
- **Second week:** chard / leaf beet, chicory for hearts, parsley
- **Third week:** chard / leaf beet, parsley
- **Fourth week:** Chinese cabbage, chicory for leaves, chervil, coriander, wild rocket

Beetroot

Beetroot plants can be set out until late July, but early in the month is more likely to yield roots of a good size for winter storage. Of all plants suitable for July planting (mostly brassicas), beetroot is the least likely to suffer pest and disease problems.

Broccoli, purple sprouting

Plants of purple sprouting broccoli may go in right at the end of July, although mid-month is a good average time, from a June sowing. As with swedes and cabbages, they often need netting against birds.

Cabbage, winter (savoy)

Savoy cabbages can be planted as late as mid-July and are easier to grow than ballheads.

Chard & leaf beet

- **Best sowing time: mid-July, indoors or outdoors, for autumn and winter harvests**
- **Other possible times: until early August indoors**
- **Chard is more colourful; leaf beet is tastier – both can be eaten raw when small**
- **Can follow a huge range of early-cropping vegetables, especially when raised as plants**

Varieties

Leaf beet is often offered with no named variety, or perhaps as 'Erbette', which is certainly of good flavour. Chard varieties have more to do with stem colour, such as 'Rhubarb Chard', with red stems, and 'Rainbow Chard' or 'Five Colours', which is usually a mix of white, yellow, orange, red and violet stems.

Sowing & planting out

Sowings in mid-July should have medium-sized leaves by late August, for harvests throughout autumn as well as winter, if it is mild. Sowings in late July still have time to establish well before winter and should start cropping by mid- to late September. Early August sowings will make smaller plants, still worthwhile for winter and spring.

Only a few plants are needed for most households, so it works well to sow in pots or modules, two or three seeds in each, for planting out three or four weeks later. A fortnight after

For summer and winter: plants of 'Rainbow Chard' in August, sown in May and picked several times, with roots that were dug up in November and potted on indoors for salads in winter (see page 160).

Easy once established

Establishing strong plants is the tricky bit, when slugs and birds are present. Once established, chard and leaf beet are among the easiest vegetables to grow and offer harvests for a long period. Their winter hardiness is also impressive, especially leaf beet – see Chapter 11, pages 160 and 164, and Chapter 15, page

sowing, if there are any seedlings in colours you do not want, you can remove them.

Spacing

For large leaves, 30cm (12") is good, or down to 15cm (6") in all directions for smaller leaves and for use in salads.

Problems

Small seedlings may be nibbled by birds, which is another reason to sow seed in pots in a protected space. Slugs are often a pest, at all stages of growth: remove any you see while picking leaves, and keep soil weed free around plants at all times.

Stems can become tough if allowed to grow large, but chard stems do look impressive and lend a beautiful element of colour and sculpture to the vegetable plot.

Older leaves tend to discolour with pale brown spots of fungal origin, but they are still edible.

Leaf miner causes rotten brown patches in leaves as the maggots chew around inside, after small flies have laid eggs on the leaves. The maggots pupate and live in soil before hatching after a few weeks, so there is no easy answer. Try growing chard in soil where nothing related was grown last year (leaf beet, beetroot, orach, tree spinach – also fat hen!) and cover new plantings with fleece or mesh.

Chicory (hearts)

- **Best sowing time: early to mid-July**
- **Other possible times: until 25 July**
- **Best sown under cover in seed trays or modules, but can also be sown direct**
- **Chicory can follow many vegetables, even onions**
- **Seedlings are susceptible to slugs, but older plants have few pests**
- **The potential rewards are high: a second crop offering delicious winter salad**

Varieties

Most sources offer chicory for hearting called 'radicchio' of one kind or another, with names such as 'Cesare' or 'Red Devil'. They are 'Palla Rossa' types, meaning 'Red Ball' – a fair

Watch for the hearts

Once plants are well established they can tolerate dry conditions in August and early September before growing strongly in autumn, when they look shiny and beautiful. Hearts develop quite late in the plants' lives and, once firm, do not stand for more than a few weeks before some of their leaves start to rot. See Chapter 11, page 161, for advice on harvesting.

description of their hearts. Alternatively, the pretty 'Lusia' has a mostly green outer heart with gorgeous yellow-and-pink inner leaves, and there are different varieties of long-leaved, deep red 'Treviso' chicories, which have exceptional frost hardiness, although their yield is poor. Chicories from Verona are good for making small hearts in late winter. There are also 'Sugarloaf' chicories, whose hearts are long, large and pale green, to harvest in autumn and store.

Sowing & planting out

The date of sowing is extremely important. Too early, in May, for example, mostly results in plants flowering rather than hearting. June and even early July sowings are on the early side for winter use, giving hearts by September or early October, while sowings in late July give plants too little time to make tight hearts.

Which leaves the middle of July. My preferred date is around 15th-23rd for winter hearts, and I suggest sowing in early July in colder areas.

Summer slugs can cause havoc among seedlings and even small plants, but are largely avoided by raising sturdy plants indoors. Sow in seed trays to prick out one seedling per pot or module, or sow three seeds per module and thin to the strongest.

Spacing

A spacing of 30-35cm (12-14") allows enough room for good-sized hearts.

Problems

Slugs are the main and, thankfully, only significant pest. Rotting of heart leaves occurs when hearts stand for too long.

Early frost of about -3°C or -4°C (27°F or 25°F), from about late October onwards, can damage hearts that have firmed up at that point. Covering chicories in November and December with a layer or two of fleece is often worthwhile. See also page 161.

'Lusia' chicory in late October (sown mid-July), with hearts well developed: they need picking at this stage or soon after, before heart leaves start to rot.

Chicory (leaves)

- **Best sowing time: late July**
- **Other possible times: early August**
- **May be sown or planted after many earlier harvests**
- **Offers salad leaves of bitter flavour in late winter and early spring**

Varieties

Almost any kind of chicory will do for leaves, including those recommended for hearts, and sowing a mix gives varied colour and leaf shape. The green leaves of 'Castelfranco', speckled with yellow and orange, are particularly pretty and frost resistant. If sown in mid-July and left unpicked, it may heart up before winter, so it is best sown no earlier than the end of July for winter harvests of leaves.

Sowing & planting out

There is a wider window of possible dates than for hearting chicories. The last week of July and first week of August are ideal; until late August is possible, especially if a cloche

Seed of mixed chicory varieties was sown in August; this photo was taken in late October, after some leaves had been picked for a month.

The same chicories in March, after a mild winter. They have already been picked of many leaves.

More of the same chicories in March: these were left unpicked and now have small hearts.

Good, bitter, healthy

The bitterness of leaf chicory takes some getting used to but is balanced, in mixes of salad leaves, by the pungency (heat) of many oriental leaves. Chicories are really worth getting to know, for their bright colours, frost hardiness, resistance to slugs and health-giving (liver-cleansing) effects.

or fleece can cover plants through winter. Sow direct in rows, or indoors then plant out.

Spacing

Allow around 15-20cm (6-8") in all directions, or, when sown in rows, aim for 30x10cm (12x4") after thinning.

Problems

Apart from slug damage to seedlings there are few pest or disease issues. Only severe winter frost may kill chicory.

Chinese cabbage

- **Best sowing time: late July**
- **Other possible times: early August, especially in milder areas**
- **Seed is best sown under cover in seed trays or modules**
- **One of the most difficult vegetables to grow successfully**
- **Chinese cabbage can follow anything harvested by mid-August**
- **Heavy hearts formed in autumn can stand until frost, then be kept indoors**

Varieties

I find that many F1 hybrids, such as 'Blues' and 'Apex', are consistent at hearting up. Other varieties, including 'Granaat' and a new red-leaved variety called 'CN 1604 F1', make less firm hearts, if at all, and are more frost hardy.

Sowing & planting out

As with hearting chicory (see page 117), there is a narrow window of opportunity for sowing, in this case from about 20 July to 5 August.

Susceptibility to pests of all kinds makes indoor sowing advisable, for planting out in mid-August after earlier crops are cleared.

Spacing

A spacing of 37cm (15") should result in plants of a fair size. Closer spacing causes earlier development of smaller hearts, which

Red Chinese cabbage 'CN 1604 F1' in October: under fleece it survived frosts of -12°C (10°F).

The same plant as pictured on previous page: many medium-sized leaves have been harvested by twisting off. There is more growth to come.

Pests, frosts, weeds

* So many pests attack Chinese cabbage that covering plants with fine mesh or fleece is almost obligatory, as soon as they are set out and even until the day of harvest. Although there are few butterflies by October, a covering at that time will protect against any early frost. Remove the cover to weed, every three weeks or so.

do not stand for use in winter. As with hearting chicory, hearts that develop too early may start to rot before it turns cold in November.

Problems

Pests are the main difficulty: caterpillars cause significant damage unless plants are covered, while you may need to patrol for slugs at planting time, with a torch and sharp knife after dusk. Flea beetles should be less evident at this time of year.

Hearts (not leaves) are susceptible to frost – see Chapter 11, page 162.

Kale

July is the best month for planting kale because it allows a preceding harvest of some other vegetable, and there is still time for good-sized plants to grow by winter. Protection from birds may be needed.

Leek

Leeks for use in late winter can be planted as late as the last week in July, but earlier plantings will give larger harvests, better resistance to leek moth and no reduction in winter hardiness.

Swede

Although swedes are commonly sown direct, planting module-raised plants is more likely to succeed and is not expensive for a vegetable that can grow to a good size, because small numbers of plants can give many meals. Aim to have planted swedes before mid-July.

WINTER HERBS

The three herbs listed here are winter-hardy biennials and fully frost hardy. They are capable of producing worthwhile amounts of leaves through winter and into spring, especially when given some basic protection from the elements, such as a cloche or cold greenhouse, or grown in a pot on the windowsill or a balcony. See Chapters 14 and 15 (pages 196, 206, 208 and 216) for details on growing them under cover in winter.

There is a huge difference between growth of coriander and chervil sown in spring, which tend to flower after only a few harvests of leaves, and the much longer life of plants sown in late summer, which start giving leaves in October and then keep going until they rise to flower from about late April.

Bankers for winter

All these herbs can be sown together in a seed tray indoors, pricked out into small pots and then transplanted outdoors in late summer, wherever a small patch of ground has been cleared of summer vegetables, such as early dwarf beans, carrots, cauliflower and salads. If they can be cloched in October, there is every chance of slow but steady harvests throughout the winter and early spring, especially in March and April. They may also survive winter without any cover at all.

Chervil & coriander

- **Best sowing time: late July to early August**
- **Other possible times: late August**
- **Seed can be sown direct in drills or in small pots to plant out or to be repotted**
- **Chervil and coriander can follow any of the many vegetables that are cleared in summer**
- **Chervil has fine flavour and elegance; coriander is as pungent as ever in winter**

Varieties

'Brussels Winter' chervil is the least inclined to flower and survives low temperatures, down to -10°C (14°F) or lower. 'Calypso' coriander is

Chervil (left) and coriander (right) in late November, from a sowing in early August in the greenhouse.

about three weeks slower to flower than most other varieties, so it crops for longer in spring, after surviving the winter.

Sowing & planting out

Both these herbs germinate more readily than parsley and also grow more quickly, so an August sowing is feasible. Late July to early August is a safe date range, to have plants of a good size to be productive in winter. Sowings in early July are at risk of flowering before winter.

Sow in small rows outside, or in pots or modules indoors. Up to five seeds per pot or module can be thinned to two or three plants, or just one if you want thick, bushy stalks.

Even after four weeks in a greenhouse, chervil often looks thin and fragile when planted out, but along with coriander it has a robustness that enables it to grow rapidly in autumn and survive in winter.

Problems

Some plants just go yellow and die at different times, and this is almost certainly due to their roots being eaten by carrot root fly maggots, or rotting at soil level from excessive winter dampness. In general, however, these are trouble-free herbs to grow in winter, especially under cover.

Better in winter than in summer

Chervil leaves have a strong taste of aniseed, which is most refreshing in winter. Both these herbs produce more winter leaves than parsley, and I add them to salad from October to May. I do not sow them in spring because they are more likely to flower than make leaves in early summer, although 'Calypso' coriander is worth a try.

Parsley

- **Best sowing time: July**
- **Other possible times: early August**
- **Seed is slow to germinate, best sown in a protected environment**
- **Parsley is high in vitamin C – a valuable winter herb**

Varieties

The main distinction is between flat-leaved and curly-leaved parsley. Named varieties of each type are offered but the differences are small.

Sowing & planting out

Sowing in early July is the best guarantee of a good-sized plant before winter, because parsley takes so long to germinate and also to grow when small. Later sowings mean that plants run out of time to establish fully before

Tidy & productive

* One or two parsley plants in 25cm (10") pots on a bright windowsill should give a good number of leaves through winter. Keep plants tidy by removing any old and yellowing leaves, and water regularly after the middle of March when growth speeds up.

winter, and then take longer to become productive after a midwinter lull.

Sow in weed-free compost in small pots, modules or a seed tray, and be patient for two to three weeks, which is the average time of emergence. Avoid using seed that is more than two years old. Thin as for chervil and coriander (see pages 121-2) and set plants out when they have about two true leaves, which may be six weeks after sowing.

Spacing

Give them room to grow, around 20-25cm (8-10") apart. Closer spacing is possible but results in thinner, more fiddly stalks and more yellow leaves at the base.

Problems

Once germinated, parsley is mostly trouble free. Outdoor plantings may suffer from carrot root fly maggots eating their roots, but this is rarely terminal.

Jobs for July

Carrots that were sown in June will benefit from some thinning in July, if you want large roots for winter. Other plants that were sown direct, such as swede and beetroot, will also need thinning.

In some years you may need to spend quite a bit of time watering in July, and little time weeding, while in other years of abundant rainfall there may be plenty of weeds and no need to water.

In either case, July is a busy month, especially when you are serious about raising new plants and clearing ground of old ones, all in good time for second crops.

Harvesting of summer crops also takes more time than in June, as courgettes, peas and beans all become increasingly productive. Sometimes, when all this is happening, it takes a real effort to remember those sowings for winter vegetables – and there are more to come in August and early September.

August-planted curly parsley (left) and flat-leaved parsley (right) on a frosty October morning; these plants went on to survive a hard winter outdoors.

Chapter 9

Sowing & planting in late summer & autumn

Still a chance to sow for winter and the hungry gap

Timing of sowings in August and September becomes more precise as the weather cools and days shorten more rapidly. Some of the dates given are therefore quite specific, to catch the best moment for a well-sized and healthy winter harvest.

Should you sow these vegetables later than recommended, the risk is that they run out of time to properly establish before winter, making them either too weak to survive or too small to be of any use. August holidays are an issue here!

Growth in August is fast, which means that bare soil, after a summer harvest is finished, can quickly be covered again with vegetables for autumn and winter harvests. It helps if you have been organised with plant raising, and have made a plan earlier in the year. By late August the plot can be as full as it was earlier in the growing season.

Beyond winter

Finally, from about the middle of September, plots develop empty spaces for hungry gap vegetables. A no-dig approach with few weeds makes it quick to remove plants after their last harvests in late summer, before sowing and planting again. I often spread some compost on newly sown soil at this point, or before setting out plants. As well as feeding the soil, this helps to conserve a little extra warmth through the colder months.

These late sowings are able to survive winter as small plants, and are then well placed to grow strongly as soon as any spring weather arrives, for harvests in April, May and June.

Right: 'Red Knight F1' mizuna in late October, sown mid-August and already picked several times.

AUGUST

	Indoors	Outdoors
Sow	**First half of month:** Chard / leaf beet, chicory for leaves, chervil, coriander, endive for hearts, land cress, oriental leaves, parsley, sorrel, wild rocket **Second half of month:** Corn salad, endive for leaves, land cress, lettuce, oriental leaves, salad rocket, salad onion, spinach, spring cabbage, winter purslane	**First half of month:** Chicory for leaves, chervil, coriander, endive for hearts, land cress, oriental leaves, parsley, sorrel, spinach, turnip / winter radish, wild rocket, winter purslane **Second half of month:** Corn salad, endive for leaves, land cress, lettuce, oriental leaves, salad onion, salad rocket, spinach, spring cabbage, winter purslane, winter radish
Plant		Chard / leaf beet, chicory for leaves, Chinese cabbage, chervil, coriander, endive for hearts & leaves, land cress, oriental leaves, parsley, sorrel, salad & wild rocket
General		Clear crop remains after last harvests of peas, beans, carrots, beetroot, salads, potatoes & onions. Look for weeds; water where necessary. Mesh carrots against carrot root fly.

August is a busy month for sowing autumn and winter salads, radishes and turnips, as well as some hungry gap vegetables.

Cabbage, spring

- **Best sowing time: mid-August outdoors, late August indoors**
- **Cabbage can follow a huge number of vegetables that finish by mid-September, except other brassicas**
- **Spring cabbage is almost a 'bonus' catch crop, growing after summer vegetables have finished and before the next year's are planted**
- **Plants are extremely frost hardy when sown at these times**

Varieties

Any of the old pointy hearting varieties are good, such as 'Durham Early' and 'Greyhound', both for greens or hearts (see box, right). Hybrids such as 'Hispi' give larger, tighter hearts but they may all mature at the same time. Another hybrid, 'Spring Hero', is the only overwintering cabbage to make a round heart, but not until May.

Sowing & planting out

Sowing cabbage in the second half of August enables plants to be established when the winter cold arrives, but without being large enough to heart up before Christmas, which may happen if they are sown too early.

Sowing is most reliable when done under cover into modules or seed trays, but outdoor sowing can also work well – one short row may be enough. Brassica seedlings prick and plant out extremely well: when planting in their final position, set them in deep enough

'Spring Hero F1' spring cabbage in early October, two weeks after planting.

In late February the plants are already starting to grow strongly; they made hearts in May.

for soil to cover their stems, which helps them to resist winter gales and frost.

Spacing

Cabbages for greens can be as close as 15-20cm (6-8") apart; spacing at 30-40cm (12-16") apart allows larger hearts to develop. Planting closer is worthwhile because some plants are often damaged in winter, or if not you can eat the extra plants as greens.

Different ways to harvest

Spring greens are close-growing cabbages that are cut for their leaves from March onwards: you can harvest every other one to make more space for the remaining plants. Then, after another month or more, there should be harvests of small hearts, not very dense but with a sweet flavour.

Problems

The usual slugs and pigeons are often nibbling away, and covering with mesh or netting is probably needed against the latter, but there are no caterpillars to contend with in spring.

Chard & leaf beet

For winter and spring use, these can be planted any time in August: if you want autumn harvests as well, aim to plant by early August, from a sowing in mid-July. This should result in plentiful leaves from September until November.

Chervil, coriander & parsley

All these herbs want planting before the end of August, and the slower-growing parsley is best planted before mid-month. They are easy to grow and worth raising in quantity.

Chicory (hearts & leaves)

Chicory for hearting is best planted before mid-August. Slugs love small plants when recently moved, so a night patrol after planting is worthwhile. Chicory for leaves can be sown direct in early August, and planted at any time in the month.

Chinese cabbage

Chinese cabbage plants are ideally set out around the middle of August, and immediately covered with fleece or fine mesh to keep insects at bay. They need watering every five days or so in dry summers, to sustain their rapid growth.

Corn salad

- **Best sowing time: late August**
- **Other possible times: early September**
- **Seed is best sown direct in the soil**
- **Corn salad (lamb's lettuce) can follow summer beans, onions, carrots and so forth**
- **Plants are small and extremely frost hardy**

Varieties

The larger-leaved 'Noordhollandse' and 'D'Orlanda' are my favourites. Another good variety is 'Vit', with smaller, darker leaves. Many others I have grown are less productive.

Sowing & planting out

Growth is slow, so, unless you live in a very mild area, plants may struggle to reach a worthwhile size from sowing later than the dates given here. On the other hand, sowing too early causes plants to mature in October, and then some of their leaves start to rot before and during winter.

Sowing direct is easiest, but may be tricky in soil with lots of weed seeds because of the length of time lamb's lettuce (corn salad) takes to germinate and grow. Sowing two or three seeds in modules for planting out, thinned to one, is also possible, but lamb's lettuce is slow to establish after planting and is one of the few vegetables I prefer to sow direct.

'D'Orlanda' lamb's lettuce in a January frost. Some plants are large enough to harvest.

Spacing

Sow in 30cm (12") rows and thin to 7cm (3"), or plant at 15x15cm (6x6").

Problems

This is one of the hardiest vegetables and is prone to little pest damage, although slugs often shelter under the leaves. Its main problem is mildew, which comes from a combination

Best in winter

The roots of lamb's lettuce are mostly near the surface in a dense mat, taking advantage of winter's high levels of moisture. Therefore, in drier autumn and spring weather they are quite likely to suffer temporary droughts, leading to mildewed leaves, which is why lamb's lettuce is best as a winter salad only.

of over-maturity and dry soil (see box, left). Sowings made in the recommended dates are unlikely to get mildew, and frequent, gentle watering is a remedy if soil is dry.

Endive (hearts & leaves)

- **Best sowing times: the first week of August is ideal for latest possible hearts; mid-August for leaf endive**
- **Other possible times: July for earlier hearts**
- **Seed is best sown in modules for planting out**
- **Endive can follow any summer vegetable**

Varieties

There are two main types of endive: scarole, with soft, broad leaves, and frizzy (also known as frisee), with serrated and more numerous leaves. For a broad-leaved scarole endive, 'Bubikopf' has the best resistance to frost. Of the frizzy endives, 'Salad King' is hardy and has long, serrated leaves, while some frizzy types, such as 'Frenzy', offer less resistance to outdoor winter weather and are better grown indoors for repeated leaf harvests. All varieties described as hearting endives can also be picked for leaves.

Sowing

For hearts in late autumn, early August is a good sowing date. For winter leaf endives, it is better to sow after the middle of August, and these plants can be picked, from October until April, as described in the box overleaf.

Sow outdoors in 30cm (12") drills, then thin to 15cm (6"), or sow two seeds per module, thin to the strongest and plant out at 20x20cm (8x8").

Planting out

Mid-August is about right to have hearts in late autumn, from sowings in late July; plantings at the end of August may also make hearts in a mild November and should also be good for winter leaves in milder areas, if picked regularly in autumn to keep plants small. Plants for winter leaves are best set out in September.

Problems

Slugs enjoy endive seedlings but are less interested in established plants. Moderate

This 'Bubikopf' scarole endive was sown in late July and is now hearting in late October.

'Salad King' in October frost of -6°C (21°F); it finally turned brown in December at -10°C (14°F).

Long harvests for endive

* Careful and regular picking of outer leaves of endive in late autumn and early spring helps to spread the harvest over a long period. Plants mostly lie dormant from December to February and may be killed by severe frost, but covering with fleece or a cloche should offer enough protection for them to survive the weather and rabbits, which adore them.

frost, below about -2°C (28°F), will damage larger and hearted plants, but smaller endives have good frost resistance, especially when protected from rain and wind.

Land cress & winter purslane

- **Best sowing time: early August**
- **Other possible times: late August**
- **Seed can be sown direct or to transplant**
- **Both these salads can follow all summer vegetables**

Hot cress & cool purslane

These hardy leaves have utterly different flavours: land cress is hot and spicy; purslane is mild and watery. They have a great ability to withstand frost but purslane offers the most winter leaves, of better quality, when protected by fleece.

Varieties

Usually there are no varietal distinctions, but note that watercress is different from land cress, suitable for autumn and spring harvests but killed by frost when grown in soil.

Sowing & planting out

Early August sowings give autumn leaves as well as winter harvests.

Both land cress and winter purslane have small seeds, so be careful not to sow too thickly. If sowing in pots or modules, I have found, after much experimenting, that one plant in each is easier to pick from than three or four, especially when aiming to keep plants growing through winter and into spring.

Five plants of land cress in a container outdoors in late November. They were sown in early August and are ready for picking many leaves.

Late August is the best date for setting out plants to have them in top condition before winter – well established and not too large.

Spacing

As for rocket (see page 136).

Problems

Land cress is a brassica, much adored by pigeons, so a net or fleece cover is often necessary. Purslane has few pest issues but is prone to lose colour in cold weather; the leaves are still edible but look more brown than green. Covering with fleece works well.

Lettuce

- **Best sowing time: late August**
- **Other possible times: mid-August in colder areas; early September in milder areas**
- **Seed is best sown in modules or trays, for planting out by late September**
- **This lettuce can follow any vegetable that finishes in late summer, except lettuce**

Varieties

Lettuce is more frost hardy than is often realised, and these varieties have extra toughness to cope with wind and rain too. The green butterhead 'Valdor', a bronze butterhead 'Marvel of Four Seasons' and a Batavian variety 'Grenoble Red' have all performed well for me outdoors, but with leaves of only average quality, owing mainly to slugs. These are also a big problem with 'Winter Density', whose sweet hearts are often marked at the base of their leaves by slug holes.

Sowing & planting out

Between 20 and 25 August is best, for a small- to medium-sized plant by Christmas.

Outdoor sowing requires care regarding slugs, but seedlings normally grow fast enough in late summer to overcome a few nibbles. Sowing can be done in modules indoors; two seeds thinned to one plant. Three weeks later they can be set out in clean soil. Be wary of slugs in a wet autumn, until plants are established.

Spacing

Aim for 10-20cm (4-8") between plants, closer than usual so that plants can give mutual support in adverse weather, and to allow for a few winter casualties.

These 'Grenoble Red' lettuces are experiencing an autumn frost; they were picked of some outer leaves and then covered with fleece over winter.

These plants become old friends

✻ Overwintering 'Grenoble Red', for picking as a *leaf* lettuce from April to June, gives an extremely long season of harvest from one sowing. Before winter, remove any old leaves at the plants' base. They should survive a winter outdoors, but a fleece cover will help. In March they can be tidied again and you should be able to pick some lower leaves weekly for nearly three months. Or plants can be overwintered in small pots and planted out in March.

Problems

Slugs are the main pest: keeping the soil well weeded helps, as does some compost spread on top, just before sowing or planting. Some protection from continual rain and damp is the main way to help winter lettuce – see advice on cloches in Chapter 14 (page 192).

Onion, salad

- **Best sowing time: late August**
- **Other possible times: early September**
- **Sow indoors or out**
- **They can follow all vegetables except onions, garlic and summer leeks**

Varieties

Nearly all varieties of salad, or spring, onion are winter hardy. 'White Lisbon Winter Hardy' is an old favourite; it can make a white bulb in May and June. Thin, upright Japanese spring onions, such as 'Ishikura' and 'Guardsman', have longer stems, but they may harbour mildew (see 'Problems' right, and page 87).

Sowing

The last week of August is best; the first week of September is possible.

Onions do not germinate well in temperatures regularly above 20°C (68°F), so indoor sowings

January: rocket and salad onions; winter purslane and land cress at the back; cloched salads behind.

Wonderful hardiness

Salad onions are exceptionally hardy and reliable, with an ability to grow in any milder weather, so they may reach a harvestable size by early April.

may suffer. Sowing in rows outdoors, with seed covered by 2cm (1") of soil, is probably the best way. If sowing in modules, up to ten seeds in each will give a worthwhile clump in the spring. Use fresh seed for best results.

Spacing

Rows of 25cm (10") can be thinned to 2cm (1") per onion. Give multi-sown modules 25cm on all sides.

Problems

Rabbits and hares love salad onions, especially in late winter when rabbit food is scarce. Otherwise they are free of most pests and diseases, with the exception that over-wintered Japanese onions appear to host onion downy mildew (see page 87), and then release it into the garden in May. 'White Lisbon' spring onions do not share this problem.

Oriental leaves

Komatsuna, leaf radish, mizuna, mustard, pak choi & tatsoi

- **Best sowing time: August**
- **Other possible times: late July and early September**
- **Oriental leaves can follow any other vegetable except other brassicas**
- **They grow fast, and offer many harvests when plants are looked after carefully**
- **Leaves have strong and varied flavours, colours and growth habits**

Varieties & types

Komatsuna, also called mustard spinach, grows extremely fast but is prone to damage

Oriental leaves sown a month earlier in August: leaf radish, land cress, pak choi, rocket, mizuna, mustards.

by slugs. There is an attractive variety called 'Red Komatsuna'.

Leaf radish grows edible roots as well as leaves. The leaves have a mildly radish flavour and grow quickly, but may suffer fungal attack in winter, surviving best as small plants.

Mizuna is easy to grow and offers plentiful harvests of mild-tasting leaves; as well as the standard green varieties, such as 'Kyoto' and 'Waido', there are red and purple-leaved mizunas. 'Red Knight F1' shows great promise for salad leaves and is as winter hardy as green varieties.

Mustard 'Red Frills' has dark red, feathery and mild-tasting leaves; 'Pizzo' leaves are pale green, crinkle-edged and of medium strength. 'Green in the Snow' has long, green and extremely pungent leaves, while 'Giant Red' is exactly that and is also pungent. Mustards are perhaps the most winter hardy of oriental leaves.

Frozen 'Red Lady F1' pak choi in late October after some leaves have been harvested.

'Pizzo' and 'Red Frills' mustard on a chilly morning in late November. They were fleeced in December.

Pak choi is vigorous and has a mild flavour, with fleshy stems, but is highly susceptible to attack by slugs. Grow it in your best soil so that it can outpace the nibbles. Some good varieties are 'Joi Choi F1' for hardy and dark green leaves, 'Red Choi' for appealing colour and a little slug resistance, and 'Mei Quing Choi F1' for small, tender leaves.

Tatsoi grows smaller than pak choi, often in pretty rosettes which can be cut as a whole vegetable; or leaves can be twisted or cut off. It is as susceptible to slugs as pak choi, but is frost hardy when pests leave it alone. Two good varieties are 'Yukina Savoy' and 'Supi', both with slightly longer stems for easier harvests of individual leaves.

Seed mixes of oriental leaves are a good idea if you want a few plants of many of these kinds of vegetable.

Sowing

For harvests in autumn, any time from early July is good, because shortening days encourage formation of leaves rather than flowers. But these fast-growing plants are susceptible to insect attack and need plenty of moisture, meaning that leaves of July sowings are often

Getting the best results

* For harvests in winter, the second half of August is a good time to sow, and even into early September. Plants will survive better and offer most winter harvests when given some protection – see Chapter 14 for more advice on protecting crops.

Many possibilities, especially with cover

The incredible range of possible leaves and their frost hardiness make these vegetables an attractive choice for winter. In mild winters they can survive without protection, but for best results it is worth covering plants with fleece or a cloche – or grow them under cover in pots and boxes.

holed by flea beetles and risk struggling in hot, dry conditions. Success is most likely from sowing in August – late enough to avoid many insects and the driest weather but early enough to allow time for growth into worthwhile plants.

Fast germination makes oriental leaves extremely satisfying vegetables to sow, either direct or in modules for planting out. The latter works better in wet summers, when slugs may eat whole rows of tiny seedlings in a night. Sow three seeds per module and thin to one or two plants.

Planting out

Beware of slugs and sometimes caterpillars too when planting oriental leaves. The latter are kept at bay with mesh or fleece, but slugs can wreak havoc underneath these covers. A very few slug pellets (one per plant) may be worthwhile in wet weather, principally for pak choi and Chinese cabbage; the poisoned slugs can later be binned.

Spacing

If you want to harvest leaves over a long period from the same plants or clumps of plants, a spacing of 20x20cm (8x8") will allow room for roots to develop and for plants to grow strongly. This works well for winter harvests, also because there is room to clear any frost or weather-damaged leaves, which allows more space for new, healthy growth to develop.

Problems

Small holes on leaves in August is a sign of flea beetles, which then diminish in autumn, so plants should be able to shrug them off by September. Slugs never go away, and any that are found while picking leaves should be removed; the same number of slugs cause more damage in winter because leaves are growing slowly.

Winter also sees some brown, fungal blotches on leaves: a purely seasonal symptom and not a sign of a plant's imminent death.

Rocket (salad & wild)

- **Best sowing time: early August for wild rocket; late August for salad rocket**
- **Other possible times: late July (wild) or early September (salad)**
- **Seed can be sown direct or to transplant**
- **Rocket can follow all summer vegetables except other brassicas**

Varieties

Wild rocket tends to come without a varietal distinction, but salad rocket has been bred into many different forms. The leaves of 'Apollo' are less lobed and larger with a milder flavour, while those of 'Skyrocket' are more serrated, but plain 'Salad Rocket' is, I find, generally as good as any other.

This row of one-year-old wild rocket in June is just four plants. Three cuts have been taken since April.

Wild & salad rocket contrasted

Compared with salad rocket, wild rocket has a different pattern of growth – lying dormant, even looking dead, in winter. Then new growth appears in early spring for a couple of months' harvests before flowering in summer. By contrast, salad rocket offers more leaves in winter, switching to mainly flowers and stems from April onwards. Both kinds give noticeably more leaves, of better quality, when afforded some protection from the weather.

Sowing & planting out

Sowings in early August make plentiful leaves before winter, and avoid the damaging flea beetles that plague July sowings. However, the best chance of salad rocket surviving extreme frost is from sowings in late August, which bring some youthful vigour into the winter. Salad rocket can be planted until the middle of September.

Module- or pot-sown seedlings want thinning to about three plants in each; if sowing direct in soil, be careful to space the small seeds quite thinly.

Spacing

Plant out at 20x20cm (8x8") or sow in rows about 25cm (10") apart and thin to 10cm (4") between plants. This gives room to pick larger leaves over a long period from each plant. Closer spacings for cutting are usually less winter hardy.

Problems

By late autumn, rocket leaves lose quality and often have brown fungal spots, which continue to occur through winter, before new growth in late winter becomes healthy again. Slugs and birds are only mildly interested in rocket, but rabbits and hares love it. Flea beetles are mostly dormant through autumn and winter, so leaves are nicely unholed.

Sorrel

- **Best sowing time: early August**
- **Other possible times: July, and until about mid-August**
- **Seed can be sown direct or in modules for transplanting**
- **Sorrel can follow any summer vegetable**

Varieties

Best for winter use is 'Broad Leaved Sorrel', the most commonly offered variety.

Sowing & planting out

Any time in late summer should work; from late July to early August ensures good-sized plants before winter, with enough roots to make new leaves in any milder weather.

Although sorrel is perennial, August-sown plants survive winter well and are useful for

A 12-year-old clump of broad-leaved sorrel in late March, in a damp spot which is much to its liking.

filling gaps. Only a few plants are needed, so sowing in small pots or modules works well, a few seeds in each, thinned to two or three. Plant in mid- to late August, after clearing peas, beans, onions, carrots and so forth. Sorrel grows well in part shade so is good to put in any damper, less sunny areas.

Spacing

Give plants room to make lots of roots – 30x30cm (12x12") is about right, or plant into a 25-30cm (10-12") pot.

Keen to grow, keen in flavour

Sorrel is extremely winter hardy and its citrus-flavoured leaves are delicious both raw and cooked. In midwinter it lies mostly dormant, with small, paler leaves, but as soon as some mildness returns in March, new healthy leaves grow rapidly, at a time when all green leaves are most welcome.

Problems

Slugs are the chief winter pest but their damage is usually cosmetic. Some browning of older leaves happens in autumn and winter, and these want removing.

Spinach

- **Best sowing time: second and third weeks of August for overwintering plants**
- **Other possible times: first or last weeks of August**
- **Seed can be sown direct or transplanted**
- **Overwintered spinach grows beautifully sweet leaves in late winter and spring**
- **Spinach can follow all summer vegetables**

Varieties

Many varieties of spinach can overwinter. Some I have found good are 'Medania', whose leaves are dense and dark green, 'Early Prickly Seed', which is quick to re-grow after a cold winter and also relatively quick to flower, 'Red Bordeaux' for colourful stems, and hybrids such as 'Tarpy' and 'Toscane'.

'Medania' spinach in November: plants survived a hard winter and cropped well in spring.

Top flavour

Although spinach leaves are often holed by slugs, the plants are really hardy and survive huge amounts of frost and winter rain. New leaves, starting in about the middle of March, are one of the few outdoor greens at that time and have a wonderful sweet flavour.

Sowing & planting out

The middle of August works well, allowing time for sufficient growth to resist slugs and inclement winter weather, yet also enabling plants to retain enough youthful vigour that any milder weather can prompt some re-growth.

Sow direct in soil, or in pots and modules, thinned to two or three plants in each. Be vigilant for slugs after planting spinach, but once established this is a hardy vegetable.

Spacing

Allow 25x7cm (10x3") in directly sown rows, or 25x25cm (10x10") for module-raised plants.

Problems

Slugs can eat spinach seedlings; raising plants in modules will help them get started. Some netting may be needed against birds, but in general this is a relatively easy vegetable for late winter and early spring harvests.

Turnip & winter radish

- **Best sowing time: first half of August**
- **Other possible times: late August for smaller roots**
- **Seed is best sown direct, then thinned**
- **These are fast-growing root vegetables**
- **Turnips and radish can follow onions, broad beans, potatoes, carrots and salads, but avoid following brassicas**

Varieties

My favourite turnips for winter are 'Milan Purple Top', a pretty flat-rooted turnip, 'Golden Ball', which is yellow with slightly denser flesh, good for storing, and 'Noir d'Hiver', whose carrot-shaped roots are most resistant to frost. 'Atlantic F1' has fewer leaves and is suitable for small spaces.

The most productive radish is 'Minnowase', with long white roots; there is also 'China Rose' and 'Black Spanish', which have round, stronger-flavoured pink and black roots respectively, and leaf radish for two harvests.

Sowing & planting out

It is possible to sow throughout the whole month, but sowings in the second half of August will have time to make only small roots, unless you live in an extremely mild area. My preferred date is around 10 August, often following a harvest of onions.

Sow turnip seeds sparingly because, although they are tiny and look so inconsequential, they all seem to germinate and subsequent growth is rapid. Some thinning in late August and early September is always worthwhile. Module-sown seed can be thinned to two or three roots each, for planting in late August.

Spacing

Sow in rows 40cm (16") apart and thin to 5-10cm (2-4") on average, using the wider

Rich flavours

Turnips and winter radish have a strong flavour, which may put you off growing them, but I urge you to have a go and see how good the flavour of home-grown roots can be, and how creamy the texture. They are two of the easiest and fastest vegetables to grow.

These 'Atlantic F1' turnips were sown on 14 August after harvesting onions. This is a fast-growing variety that resists autumn frosts but is not hardy in severe winters.

spacing for larger roots. Modules can be planted at 25x25cm (10x10").

Problems

Maggots of the cabbage root fly tunnel around and make roots unattractive, although they are still edible once the damaged parts have been sliced off. One way to prevent this is by covering plants with mesh or fleece, which will also keep pigeons and butterflies at bay.

Jobs for August

August is one of the busiest months if you want to fit in many of these winter sowings and plantings, at the same time as continuing with picking beans and all the summer vegetables.

If you have kept on top of weed growth, you should find that clearing crop residues before re-sowing or planting does not take too long. I find that harvested onions, for example, leave a clean soil behind them, which I smooth down simply by *walking or dancing on the often dry soil*, to break up any lumps of compost and push down soil that has been loosened by pulling onions.

Weeds should be under control by now, many of them discouraged from germinating by the shade of vegetable plants. Do keep looking for weeds – it only takes a few minutes to pull out a few plants that might otherwise set seed and cause you much grief next spring.

Watering may also be necessary, but becomes easier as the month progresses and some dampness returns to the air. Rain and warmth in late August and September can often make it feel like a second spring, with all the summer sowings well placed to take advantage of a late burst of growing weather. By the end of August, only winter salads remain to be sown.

Tidying up

* Clear all remains of finished crops as soon as a last harvest is taken, to be ready for second sowings and plantings. Slug numbers are reduced when all old leaves and stems are removed to a compost heap.

SEPTEMBER

	Indoors	Outdoors
Sow	Corn salad, oriental leaves in first ten days, salad onion. Also winter salads for cloched & indoor growing (see Chapter 15)	Corn salad, garlic (see October), oriental leaves in first ten days; broad beans & mustard as green manure
Plant	Some salads & vegetables for winter leaves (see Chapter 15)	Corn salad, endive for hearts & leaves, garlic (see October), land cress, lettuce, oriental leaves, salads for cloches, salad & wild rocket, sorrel, spinach, spring cabbage, winter purslane, salad onion
General	Sow first salads for winter leaves, after clearing summer vegetables.	Sow mustard green manure if you have bare spaces.

September is part summer and part autumn, but more of the former. A few last sowings may be made outdoors, and a lot of plantings can happen, in the first week especially. At the month's end there are some vegetables to plant whose harvests will not happen until the spring.

- September plantings are for two different seasons of harvest.
- Plantings in the first half of the month should provide leaves for salads and cooking by late autumn, then through winter in small amounts and more significantly in early spring, especially when covered with fleece or a cloche.
- Plantings after mid-month are of vegetables to overwinter as small plants, but with well-developed root systems. These roots enable them to grow quickly in early spring, providing harvests from April to June, at a time when most spring sowings are still growing and are not ready to eat.

Other September plantings are made under cover, mostly late in the month and for salad; these are covered in Part 6.

Corn salad

Corn salad (lamb's lettuce) can be sown until about 10 September, but every day of sowing later will result in the winter harvest being postponed by about a week, and it will probably be smaller too. Plants can be set out at the end of September and take a few weeks to settle in.

Endive

Endive planted in early September may make a small heart, and it needs planting by mid-September for winter and spring harvests. Harvesting a few outer leaves should also be possible in November, if the autumn is mild.

Green manures

Mustard, leaf radish, mizuna

- **Best sowing time: early to mid-September**
- **Other possible times: August for leaf radish, late September for mustard**
- **Either sow broadcast, lightly raked in, or in 25cm (10") rows**
- **Seed can be covered with a light dressing of compost**

- **Mustard is a fast-growing plant and is usually killed by frost**
- **Leaf radish and mizuna can be hoed off if they survive winter**
- **Sow seed sparingly, about 5cm (2") apart, or more thickly for later sowings**

These plants are useful if you don't want to keep planting up the post-harvest bare spaces with vegetables. They pull in energy from the sun and add it back to the soil, smothering many weeds at the same time.

Mustard is killed by any hard frost of about -5°C (23°F) or lower. By spring, all that remains are some strawy stems on the surface and

Broad beans – both green manure & salad leaf

Broad beans can be sown as a green manure in September, in rows about 30cm (12") apart and beans set every 10cm (4"). Keep them weeded, and from about the middle of October you can take a harvest of bean tops for salad, by pinching out the top 3-5cm (1-2") of growth. New growing points will then develop lower down and harvests of shoots can continue all winter in mild areas, but plants are usually killed by frost at some point.

Leaf radish in October, still growing rapidly: the leaves and roots are good to eat if wanted.

decomposing roots underneath: rake off the debris of old stems, remove any weeds, and soil is then ready to sow or plant. If you spread some compost on top of the mustard seed in September, your soil will be in a lovely friable condition by spring.

Mizuna and **leaf radish** are two fast-growing oriental leaves, which can be grown both for green manure and to eat if needed. Sow at about twice the usual rate, as early in September as possible.

Land cress, rocket (salad & wild), winter purslane

Early September is the best time for planting these, to have a fair chance of salad leaves in the winter half of the year. Later plantings until the end of September can be covered with fleece or a cloche to help them grow – see Chapter 14, pages 191-2.

Lettuce, spring cabbage & salad onion

These vegetables are not expected to grow large before winter, so planting them in the last week of September is a good time – so that they have just enough warmth and light to establish roots and grow a little before winter sets in. Cabbage probably wants covering with netting against pigeons, lettuce may be fleeced from about December, and spring onions usually stand all weathers.

Oriental leaves

Komatsuna, leaf radish, mizuna, mustard, pak choi & tatsoi

Oriental leaves can still be sown in the first week of September and should reach a worthwhile size before winter. Although these sowings may not give many harvests in autumn, they should be well placed to survive winter outdoors, especially if protected with fleece or a cloche, from the middle or end of October (see Chapter 14).

All oriental vegetables for leaves can be planted outdoors in September, preferably by mid-month. They survive outdoors in temperatures as low as -5°C (23°F), but below that some plants may be lost and fleece or a cloche is worthwhile.

Salads, winter

Indoor sowings of salads for growing in greenhouses, polytunnels and conservatories are explained in Chapter 15 (page 202 onwards). Most of them are made in September.

Many kinds of salad plants can be set out in about the middle of September, from late August sowings, then covered with cloches in October.

Sorrel & spinach

Early in the month is an excellent time for setting out spinach plants to crop in the spring. Later plantings will do better for being covered with fleece or a cloche. Sorrel needs planting by the first week of September, but August is better.

Jobs for September

This month is more about harvesting than new planting, but I hope the list in the previous pages encourages you to realise the possibilities for keeping your plot productive until the season's end. Remember to keep pulling any small weeds, which would otherwise grow and mature fast, at a time of year when growth is still rapid.

OCTOBER

	Indoors	Outdoors
Sow	Carrots, possibly mizuna (see Chapter 15 for both)	Garlic, broad beans
Plant	Winter salads (see Chapter 15)	
General	Clear last of summer plants, water. Finish planting winter salads.	Weed to have soil clean before winter. Cover salads with cloches.

Daylight levels by the middle of October are equivalent to those in late February, and this is often an end point for significant new growth in much of Britain. There are only two outdoor sowings/plantings to make, but still several plantings to finish indoors.

Beans, broad

- **Best sowing time: mid- to end of October**
- **Other possible times: early November**
- **Seed is best sown into holes made by a dibber**
- **Can be covered with a dressing of compost or well-rotted manure**

Varieties

The classic variety for overwintering is ‘Aquadulce Claudia’, which grows long pods of fine-tasting, pale white beans. I have also found ‘Masterpiece Green Longpod’ to survive winter conditions; its beans are green and dense, smaller than ‘Aquadulce’.

Sowing

I like to have plants about 5cm (2") high, certainly no more, by Christmas, because frost damages the stems if they are too long in winter. Sowing in late October or very early November is good for most of Britain, but sow earlier or later if your climate is either much milder or colder than average.

It is quicker to dib individual holes than to draw out deep drills, because broad beans like to be put in 5-7cm (2-3") down; or sow a little less deep and immediately cover with 3cm (an inch or so) of compost or well-rotted manure.

Spacing

Sowing in rows of 40cm (15") across beds, with seed 10-15cm (4-6") apart, allows access between the rows for picking pods.

Problems

If mice abound, they may eat newly sown seeds: mixing seed with grated garlic can deter them. In December, just after emergence, birds such as rooks may pull the newly germinated seedlings out. By the time you notice this it is too late to remedy, so covering the bed with cloche hoops and some netting or mesh is worthwhile, from the time of sowing until about early March.

Miraculous multiplication

Sometimes by early March the bean bed looks sadly diminished, as some or several plants have died in winter. However, do not despair: all plants that survived the winter will make several new stems from their base during March and April. So it is often worth waiting for new growth rather than pulling out the straggly survivors of winter.

Sowing broad beans

1. Dibbing holes to sow broad beans. Holes are 5cm (2") deep and about 10cm (4") apart.
2. Sowing broad bean seed. One or two seeds per hole is fine.
3. Filling sown holes with the dibber to push and pull loose soil.
4. Covering the bed with compost straight after sowing the seed.

Garlic

- **Best planting time: late September or early October**
- **Other possible times: until Christmas**
- **Cloves are best planted with a dibber**
- **After planting, compost or well-rotted manure can be spread on top**

Varieties

There is now an increasing choice of varieties available and I recommend you read the small print to see which characteristics you prefer. There are two types of garlic: softnecks, which often grow larger and store a little less well, and hardnecks, which have flowering stalks that can be cut out and eaten in late April and May.

Planting

The last week in September and early October are best, after last harvests of runner beans, beetroot, courgettes or summer salads, for example. Garlic is extremely hardy and bulbs planted in autumn grow larger than from a spring planting.

This garlic, despite emerging only in January, is well established by late February.

In late May the plants are almost fully grown and will be harvested in about four weeks.

Break up the bulbs and separate larger cloves for planting, smaller ones for eating. Dib holes and set cloves 5cm (2") deep, or plant in more shallow holes and cover the bed with 3cm (1") of compost or well-rotted manure.

Spacing

Rows of 30-40cm (12-16") and cloves 12-15cm (5-6") apart give good-sized bulbs. Plant a few of the smaller cloves closer together, for pulling as green garlic in late April and May.

Problems

White rot is a problem you may encounter, and by the time you see it, with leaves yellowing rapidly in spring, there is nothing to do except pull the infected bulb to burn or bin, and then remember not to grow any alliums in that bed or area for at least five years.

Early signs of spring

Seeing new growth after Christmas is a great tonic. Garlic puts down a lot of roots in late autumn and winter; at first it seems that nothing much is happening, until, with the first hint of mildness in the new year, bright spears of green suddenly appear.

Sometimes frost may cause growing cloves to rise above the surface: bulbs should still develop but will appreciate earthing up with soil or compost. You can prevent this another year by planting a little deeper.

Orange flecks of rust appear on leaves from April to June, mostly when the soil is dry; watering from late April to early June is often worthwhile.

Jobs for October

Some soil can now be prepared for winter where summer vegetables have been cleared, and any weeds removed, leaving a bare surface between the areas where winter vegetables are growing.

I have found that a surface dressing of compost or manure at this stage offers plenty of food for worms and other soil organisms – to keep them in good health and ready, in a few months, to start the growing season again. The organic matter is broken up by frost in winter.

Apart from this, and the plantings described on the previous pages, October (and November) is a month of picking and storing. And again for November, as explained in Part 4.

PART 4

Winter harvests

Chapter **10**

Winter harvests calendar

From July to June – winter's long reach

Knowing when vegetables are ready to be picked is as important as growing them in the first place. With experience, you can look at a plant and assess its readiness; until then, use this harvests calendar as a framework to help you get the most out of what you grow.

The list covers almost 12 months, from the summer and autumn harvests to store for later use, through winter itself, to harvests that are possible in the hungry gap of spring – mostly from overwintered vegetables. These have great value at a time when the vegetable plot has more growing plants than harvestable ones.

SUMMER AND AUTUMN, for storing

The vegetables to harvest from July to November are mostly winter staples to store – always available, indoors, and ready for eating. The harvesting dates and details given in this chapter and in Chapter 11 are complemented by advice on storage in Part 5.

June/July

Even as summer is just beginning, there are some harvests happening for winter. The first one, garlic, is also one of the longest keepers, with a flavour changing from mild to pungent.

Garlic

Watch for yellowing of the leaves of garlic, which often starts in June. Sometimes this is increased by rust on the leaves, which causes early ripening: a rule of thumb is that leaves of half yellow and half green suggest you should dig the bulbs, from late June to about mid-July. Don't wait for them all to go yellow.

August

Three more winter staples can be gathered to store in the heat of August, and they will keep better if there is some sun to dry them before storage. This is especially true for onions.

Potatoes (second early), onions & shallots

Second early potato varieties start to show yellow after late July and are ready to pull or dig out when most of their leaves are no

Right: 'Sanguina' beetroot in October, sown in modules and planted in July after lettuce.

longer green. If blight is causing the leaves to go brown, they want harvesting immediately.

Onions and shallots show ripeness by some stems falling over, with a yellowing as well. You can lift them with a trowel at this point and bend all their necks, usually in early August for onions and a fortnight earlier for shallots. If mildew has infected the leaves, you need to harvest in July.

September

At the tail end of summer there is plenty to eat and still not much to gather for winter. The main harvests will begin in October and November.

Potatoes (maincrop) & beans for drying

Maincrop potatoes, if not blighted, should continue growing through August and then mature in September, with a yellowing of their leaves: proceed as for second earlies (see 'August', page 148).

Beans for drying will have many pods crisp by now: you can either pick some at this stage, or wait a fortnight and pick all pods into separate dry and non-dry containers.

October

This is a busy month in every way, but harvesting takes priority when time is limited, so that vegetables can then be stored in top condition.

Beans, carrots, winter squashes

Beans for drying should have dry or mostly dry pods by early October.

Carrots for winter use can be harvested from about the middle of October, preferably in colder weather so that they keep well.

'Blue Ballet' and 'Orange Hokkaido' squash: the dry stems show readiness for harvest.

The leaves of winter squash are mostly mildewed and fading by early October, with squashes visible and ripening – one hopes – in some late sunshine, before being cut off the stem and brought indoors before any frost of about -2°C (28°F) or more.

November

Some of November's harvests are optional: hardy vegetables such as celeriac, beetroot and turnips can be left outside, but are often safer indoors – from animals as much as from frost.

Carrots, beetroot, celeriac, turnips, winter radishes, endive hearts, Chinese cabbage & chicory hearts & roots to force

November is the best month for harvesting carrots to store, as long as carrot root fly maggots have not entered the roots. If half-eaten already, they are best trimmed and eaten fresh.

'Noir d'Hiver' turnip is long, thin, tasty and more frost resistant than other varieties.

Beetroot, celeriac, turnips and winter radishes may be harvested as late as the end of November or early December if frosts are not severe, because they can all stand frosts down to about -5°C (23°F). Rows of roots can also be earthed up, helping to keep frost and even rats off them.

Hearts of endive, Chinese cabbage and some chicory do not resist frost and are best covered with a double layer of fleece in cold weather. You need to choose whether to keep them outside, at risk from frost and slugs, or harvest them to store, where they will lose some of their freshness.

Roots of forcing chicory are best dug out from late November, before frost becomes too severe. They can be trimmed and potted up, or kept in a sack until wanted for forcing (see pages 160-1).

WINTER – mostly fresh harvests

By the year's end, reduced temperature and minimal daylight make all new growth extremely slow. Therefore most harvests are of vegetables that have done most of their growing already, and that stay in good condition during cold weather and short days.

Fortunately there are quite a few such vegetables, to add to all those that have already been stored. Even some salads can be found outdoors, although after Christmas this becomes meagre, with indoor salads really coming into their own during the first quarter of the new year (see Part 6).

December

Now is the time to lift the rest of your root vegetables for storage, although others, such as parsnips, keep best in the ground. And even in December there are some welcome leafy greens to be picked.

Final harvest of roots to store: celeriac, radishes, turnips & beetroot, also chicory roots to force

If turnips, radishes and beetroot have not yet been stored, they want harvesting before any hard frost (-5°C/23°F or lower). By contrast, the roots listed below are more hardy and can stay outdoors all winter. Celeriac is frost hardy but keeps so well in store, where it is also safe from wild animals, that I recommend harvesting it before winter really sets in.

Chard, leaf beet & spinach

These plants can survive a certain amount of freezing weather but lose quality on larger, outer leaves, so pick plants hard in December to leave a small core of leaves, which should re-grow in late winter.

'Golden Detroit' beetroot from one module, sown late June and planted after lettuce.

Harvest when needed: leeks, parsnips, swedes, Jerusalem artichokes, Brussels sprouts, kale, savoy & some ballhead cabbage

These are the main outdoor harvests of the next four months. All except autumn varieties of leeks (see page 96) should survive all weathers, though there may be some damage to Brussels sprouts in extremely low temperatures.

Salad: corn salad, land cress & last chicory hearts; leaves indoors

Any remaining hearts of chicory want gathering before moderate frost, but leaves such as corn salad (lamb's lettuce), winter purslane and land cress will survive a fair amount of freezing – especially lamb's lettuce. Other salads, such as oriental leaves, sorrel, wild and salad rocket and endive, and also herbs such as parsley, coriander and chervil, will continue offering small harvests until frosts become regular.

January to February

What we can pick outdoors at this time of year depends on the weather – so variable from one winter to the next. Here are some general guidelines and possibilities.

Outdoor harvests similar to December

A few harvests can be made in frozen weather. Plants such as cabbage, kale and Brussels sprouts may look less handsome, but they taste just as good when trimmed for the table. Leeks such as 'Bandit' should keep in good condition and will even grow a little in any mild weather. An undug, surface-composted soil will freeze less hard than a dug soil, making it easier to harvest parsnips, leeks, Jerusalem artichokes and swedes.

Chard, leaf beet & spinach in mild winters

If frosts are only slight, a few new leaves are possible, but their quality will be rather poor, often with small slug holes.

'D'Orlanda' lamb's lettuce, sown late August, in early January after hard frosts in December.

Salads: corn salad, chicory leaves, other outdoor leaves in mild winter only; more indoors, including chicons

The main outdoor salad is lamb's lettuce, able to survive hard frost and significant snow cover. There may also be some new leaves of land cress and winter purslane, and indoor leaves start to make significant new growth after about the middle of February. Chicons grown in the house can be harvested through January and February, without even needing to put a coat on!

A hint of spring

March and April are mostly about winter, in terms of vegetables to harvest, but there is some exciting new growth of salad leaves and from perennial plants such as rhubarb.

March

March is the first of two transition months when some significant new growth is possible thanks to increasing light levels, even though temperatures may often still be low.

Winter staples continue

Remaining leeks grow noticeably larger, kale makes more new leaves of better quality and savoy cabbages increase the size of their hearts. Chard, leaf beet and spinach grow again, just slowly at first. Parsnips and swedes are often at their sweetest.

Rhubarb stems; purple sprouting broccoli offers its first shoots

Early varieties of rhubarb can yield some small pickings in March, even when there may be a little frost damage around their leaf margins.

The first shoots of purple sprouting broccoli are an exciting taste of spring. When they are ready depends on both the temperature and the variety grown.

Salads: new growth after mid-March outdoors on all plants that have survived; rapidly increasing harvests indoors; more chicons

At some point in March you should notice some larger and healthier leaves appearing on lamb's lettuce, land cress, winter purslane, spinach, parsley, chervil, coriander and both salad and wild rocket. Salad plants growing indoors often become abundant after about the middle of March, by which time daylight levels are equivalent to those of late September. The last harvests of chicons happen in March.

April – the transition month

Many winter roots and brassicas now start to make flower stems, and most of these flower stems are edible. New harvests of autumn-sown cabbage come ready at some point, depending on the weather. The last few leeks are really useful, spinach and chard can be relatively abundant, and salad leaves are possible on both overwintered plants and on spring-sown ones by the end of April.

Parsnips, Brussels sprouts, cabbage & kale

These vegetables can be harvested until about the middle of April, and flowering stems of the brassicas are good to eat after that – especially the first ones, more juicy and tender.

Purple sprouting broccoli & leeks can be prolific

Sprouting broccoli should be plentiful in April and may need harvesting twice a week. Leeks make lot of new growth and can double in size in a few weeks, before flowering any time from late April to the middle of May.

Cauliflower sown last June, the first spring cabbage & salad onions

Keep a close eye on cauliflower plants for developing curds, and on spring cabbages for any pale hearts – or eat them as greens, before hearting. Salad (spring) onions can be picked at whatever size you like them.

Spinach, chard & leaf beet

Overwintered plants really start to flourish in April, their extensive root systems enabling many new leaves to grow.

Perennials come into their own

April should see plenty of rhubarb and some good shoots of seakale, blanched or green, and the first spears of asparagus at the month's end.

'Spring Hero F1' spring cabbages putting on lots of healthy growth after a warm April.

Salads: more leaves outdoors, abundance indoors

Outdoor salads grow more strongly now, from overwintered plants such as lamb's lettuce, land cress, chicory, endive, rocket, sorrel and

Chervil, parsley, leaf radish and 'Red Frills' mustard in April after being frozen many times in winter. They were all sown in late summer and early autumn, and have been harvested of many leaves, weekly or fortnightly since November.

oriental leaves (giving flowers too), and herbs such as parsley, coriander and chervil. There should be a huge abundance of indoor leaves.

The hungry gap

Here are the vegetable year's two most enigmatic months, when it may feel like summer and yet the garden is almost bare of harvests, in May especially.

May & June

This is a potentially frustrating season because winter vegetables have finished and new sowings are mostly not yet mature. Harvests at this time come from autumn plantings of overwintered vegetables, a relative abundance of perennial vegetables and also from new plantings of salad, some of which have been fleeced or cloched.

'Tall Sugar Pea' shoots ready to pick in May, from plants sown early March and covered with fleece.

Last purple sprouting broccoli, chard, leaf beet, spinach & leeks

Until mid-May, all of these vegetables can yield good pickings. Then they go into full flowering mode, with few new leaves or new tender shoots of broccoli.

Spring cabbage, cauliflower, sorrel & salad onions

From overwintered plants there should be plenty to eat now.

Green garlic, bean tops & the first baby pods of broad beans

These delicious tastes of spring are the result of many months' slow growth. Tops of broad beans can be pinched off when plants are in full flower.

New sowings

Fast-growing vegetables such as radishes and spinach can be sown from late March, for picking in May, especially if they are covered with fleece or a cloche. Even beetroot can be ready by late May, from indoor sowings of 'Boltardy' in modules in late February, planted under fleece in April. From early June It may even be possible to harvest peas from early sowings.

Perennial vegetables: rhubarb, asparagus, wild plants

Spring is a great season for harvests of perennials, including hedgerow plants such as wild garlic and nettles, whose well-developed roots provide rapid new growth at a time when annuals are often only just germinating.

Salads

Overwintered salads now come to an end by flowering, mostly before the middle of May. By that time, new sowings of lettuce leaves, spinach and pea shoots can be ready (see Chapter 11), if they have been sown in February indoors or March outdoors, and covered with fleece or a cloche when sown or planted. Wild rocket is productive in May, and there are also wild leaves to gather such as dandelions, fat hen, nettle tops and cleavers.

Winter & hungry gap vegetables A–Z

The main harvests for eating in winter and spring

I have categorised these vegetables into three types, according to their main period of harvest:
Summer and autumn, for storing through winter: S
Winter itself: W
Spring, the hungry gap: G

There are 45 vegetables listed, with 13 for storing, 27 for picking in winter, and 24 for harvests in the hungry gap (some vegetables overlap in adjacent categories).

The majority of these harvests are from an outdoor plot, but I also suggest which vegetables can profitably be given some protection, making it possible to enjoy more harvests in midwinter. These are mainly salad plants, and there is more information on growing them in Chapter 15.

Asparagus G

Spears of asparagus first appear around the middle of April in most parts of Britain – St George's day on 23 April is a likely time for the first harvest, which then continues until late June. This makes asparagus a valuable vegetable because there are not so many fresh greens to harvest at that time, and spears can be picked or cut regularly, just above ground level and when 20-30cm (8-12") high.

Beans, broad W, G

From closely spaced October sowings (see Chapter 9, page 143) it is possible to have a small harvest of the top inch or so (2-3cm) of stem, for eating as winter salad or greens, even in frosty weather. New shoots continue to appear through the spring. By June, on plants whose tops have not been picked until May, there should be the first tender pods.

Beans for drying S

Pods can either be picked as and when they dry, or all at the same time on a dry day in late September or early October. Use a second bucket for any less dry beans, which can be laid out somewhere with warmth and air to finish drying. After shelling beans out of dry pods, leave them on a tray indoors for a week or so to completely dry, then they can be stored in jars and should keep for more than a year if necessary.

Right: 'Red Russian' kale in February. The leaves are hardy and yet tender to eat, even in salads.

Beetroot S, W, G

Beetroot is a reliable winter staple from harvests in November and December, before temperatures fall below about -4°C (25°F). When kept cool, the roots should be usable until early spring, for delicious soups and grating in salads. You can also sow 'Boltardy' beetroot indoors in modules in February, for planting outdoors under fleece in April, to harvest from late May. Also, a few roots potted into compost and kept in a light, mostly frost-free environment will send out new leaves for salad in late winter and early spring.

These sprouts should stand for many weeks with the ageing outer leaves removed.

Broccoli, purple sprouting G

Except in a severe winter with frosts of around -12°C (10°F) or lower, broccoli should sprout from some time in March until the middle of May. Some varieties crop earlier than others, but on average the main harvest period is from late March to early May, as long as pigeons can be kept at bay. The first shoots are fat and stumpy, then later harvests longer and thinner, with stems that are tender and of an excellent flavour, reminiscent of asparagus. By May the thin sprouts become a little woody and the buds open readily into yellow flowers, at which point the plants are best pulled up and chopped for compost, before they take too much moisture and goodness from the soil.

Brussels sprouts W

Winter varieties of Brussels sprouts should stand until April, when their flowering shoots are even more delicious than the sprouts. Sprout tops are also tasty, but harvesting these, from November onwards, will stop any further development of the stem and new sprouts. Winter harvests of sprouts vary in quality – according to your success in growing them, the weather and the variety chosen. Buttons are mature when the large leaves coming out of the stalk closest to them start to yellow – removing these leaves and stems before they rot in proximity to the sprouts helps keep buttons in good condition until you want them. Severe frost of about -10°C (14°F) or more may cause sprouts to rot, and this is not always apparent from buttons' healthy-looking outside leaves.

Cabbage, spring G

Depending on the variety grown, small hearts of spring cabbage develop from the middle of April until June. Before that, whole plants can be cut as spring greens, or outer leaves can be picked off for greens, which allows plants to continue growing.

Cabbage, winter (ballhead) S, W

Ballhead white and red cabbages make tight hearts in autumn, but sometimes these mature in September and are then more difficult to keep in good condition through winter. Ideally you would hope to cut them as dense hearts from late October to early December, before any moderate frost. Two varieties, 'January King' and 'Tundra', with crinkly leaves like savoy cabbage, are more hardy and heart up later, for harvesting straight off the plot from December to March – an easier option.

Cabbage, winter (savoy) W

Savoys are incredibly hardy, and some varieties also have the ability to grow strongly in

March and early April, when their hearts swell with bright green leaves. So the harvesting period is long, and most value comes from growing late varieties to harvest in March and early April, when vegetables are scarcer than in midwinter – as long as you can keep pigeons off your plants.

Carrot S

Carrot root fly is an issue here because it is quite likely that a few of their larvae are in some carrots at the time of harvest, from mid-October to the end of November. They then continue to eat away when carrots are being stored, and you may be shocked to see lots of damaged roots by February: see pages 110-11 for ways of keeping the flies at bay before harvest. Carrots can also be pulled fresh in winter, but I would try it only on sandy, free-draining soil with few slugs: cover them in November with straw and/or fleece to give protection when the temperature falls below about -3°C (27°F). Then they can be harvested as needed until early April.

Cutting a frozen head of 'Ormskirk' savoy cabbage in January.

Cauliflower, spring G

A difficult harvest to achieve. If you can bring large plants through winter, they will develop curds from March to May, at an imprecise time that depends on the weather and, mainly, the variety grown. Keep watching plants, ready with your knife to catch the best moment: developing curds can be covered with old leaves to help keep any spring frosts at bay.

This head of 'Graffiti' cauliflower is a late June rather than spring harvest. Seed was sown indoors in late February and plants were set outdoors, under fleece in April.

Or, more easily, sow seeds indoors in late February to plant under fleece in April: these should make curds in June.

Celeriac S, W

Roots of celeriac store well from harvests in November and December, before the temperature drops too low: I once harvested some roots after a long December night of -6°C (21°F) and they were fine, but that is close to the limit. Trim off all leaves but leave some soil around the bottoms of roots to help them keep moist through winter. In mild areas they can stay in the soil until needed.

Chard W, G

Chard is half-hardy and may survive until May, when it develops graceful flowering stems. There are few new leaves of decent quality between December and February, unless plants are covered with fleece or a cloche. It is worth picking off all decaying outer leaves (and slugs) in early March to reveal the healthy new growth, which should then give increasing harvests for a couple of months. Remove any slugs you notice when picking leaves.

You can also dig up chard roots in November to pot on in a greenhouse or conservatory, where they will grow small salad leaves through winter, as for beetroot.

Chervil W

Chervil is hardy to frost but loses leaf quality in constant rain and cold, so it is worth putting a cloche over plants, or bringing a pot inside, where it may surprise you with its growth. Outdoor harvests will be small in winter, but if plants survive in good health there will be some healthy leaves in April.

Chicons W, in darkness

Chicory roots grown outdoors want harvesting before moderate frost of -4 or -5°C (25-23°F). Late November until Christmas is often a good time: any earlier and roots may not have been exposed to enough cold for initiation of chicon growth. Use a fork or spade to extricate as much of the root as possible – any fragments left behind will be annoying weeds next year. Trim off all leaves – a few inner ones are edible, although bitter. You will be left holding a rather unattractive root.

A root of celeriac harvested in October and ready to store through winter.

Roots of 'Tardiva' chicory in April. These were harvested in December and packed in compost.

Roots can be placed in 25-30cm (10-12") pots – as many as three or four in each if on the small side – or in buckets, with any kind of compost or soil around them, whose function is to retain moisture rather than provide goodness. Pack in the roots so that their tops, out of which chicons will grow, are just above the compost or soil, which can be lightly watered every two or three weeks. Another possibility is to place roots in polythene sacks or bags, unsealed.

Chicons grow best in complete darkness, making them sweet, yellow and densely folded. At room temperature (16-20°C/61-68°F) they may be ready in three weeks; at temperatures of around 10°C (50°F), in up to eight weeks. Most roots grow several chicons, although some grow just one large one. Cut or twist off the largest first when 10-15cm (4-6") high; others can be harvested every few days for up to a month, by which time they will have more stem and may also be harbouring some aphids, which can be washed off before use.

Harvests can be staggered if you have somewhere to keep roots cool and frost free; bring a few at a time into the warmth of your house.

After four weeks or so of harvest, new chicons become small and thin. Roots are best composted at this point, after a final harvest.

Chicory hearts S

These can be harvested fresh until the first frosts of -4°C (25°F) or so. If winter stays exceptionally mild, they may stand outside in a less hearted state. Radicchio and sugarloaf hearts tolerate only slight frost, so need cutting in November or possibly December, before frosts of -3 or -4°C (27-25°F). Trim off decayed outer leaves and put in polythene bags, kept as cool as possible until needed. Plants that have not made firm hearts at this time may survive winter outdoors – sugarloaf especially; immature hearts can then be

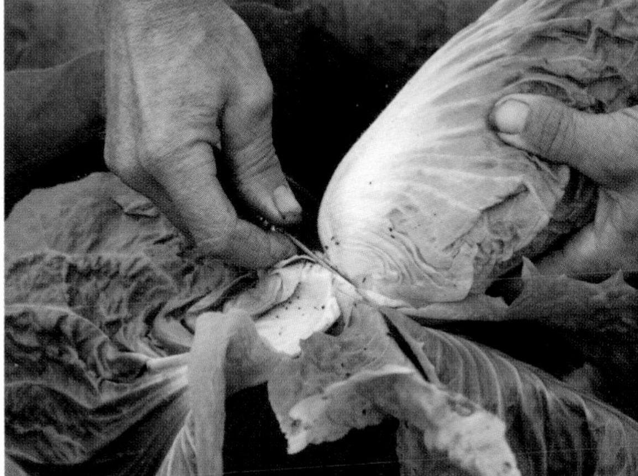

Harvesting a heart of sugarloaf chicory in late autumn. The decayed outer leaves are trimmed.

picked for salad at any time, or they can be dug up as for endive hearts – see overleaf.

Chicory leaves W, G

Small plants of chicory grown for leaves should survive winter outdoors, but harvests of new leaves will be small, unless they are covered with fleece or a cloche. Plants can be tidied of

Picking outer leaves of 'Palla Rossa Romea' chicory, which is actually a variety for hearting.

any eaten or damaged leaves in early March and there should then be new harvests until May. Leaves are rather bitter, but they are welcome at a time when outdoor salad is scarce.

Chinese cabbage S

This is a vegetable for early winter only, from hearts cut in October and November, as long as they have been protected from caterpillars and autumn frosts until that point. Many outer leaves may be slimy and slug-eaten at harvest time, but can be trimmed off to reveal a sound core of pale, crunchy inner leaves.

Coriander W, G

Coriander is more associated with summer than winter leaves, but it is actually extremely hardy, living for much longer when sown in late summer than when sown in the spring. Steady growth of leaves, in any interludes between frost, accelerates in March and April before flowering in May, when harvests can still continue for a while. Giving plants some winter protection is worthwhile, and a window box or pot on the windowsill works well.

Corn salad W

Although lamb's lettuce can be harvested in the autumn, I suggest leaving it for winter, when it may be your only outdoor salad leaf. From plants sown in late August and early September, rosettes of eight to ten leaves can be cut at any time in winter. If you are careful to cut above soil level, there will be some regrowth from the same stem. This becomes more prolific after mid-March, and until flowering stems appear around the middle of April, at which point plants are best removed by cutting the main stem just below soil level.

Endive hearts S

This is similar to Chinese cabbage (see above), suitable for harvesting in early winter only, as hearts are so easily damaged by frost. Keep an eye on the weather forecast: if frosts are only slight, no more than -2°C (28°F), hearts should survive, especially if fleeced, and can be harvested by about late November, then kept for about three weeks in a bag in the fridge or a cool shed. Alternatively, dig plants up with a small rootball of soil and keep them in boxes in a shed until needed; 'Bubikopf' will even survive being frozen after digging up, if frost can enter the shed, and its leaves become slightly blanched in the absence of light.

Twisting outer leaves of 'Bubikopf' endive in November, from plants sown in August.

Endive leaves W, G

Late August and early September sowings of endive plants, which have not hearted and are kept small by some picking of outer leaves, can tolerate a lot of frost, but they do not like it cold and wet. Some protection should give small pickings of winter leaves, becoming more abundant after the middle of March, until plants flower in May.

Garlic S, G

Garlic stores well, from the very first winter harvest in late June or early July. Watch for yellowing of the leaves and harvest while some are still green: if you wait for a complete yellowing, the bulbs' outer skins will be starting to rot and they may keep less well. Be careful to lift bulbs undamaged: use a trowel to gently prise them out, rub or shake most of the soil away from the roots, then hang in bunches somewhere airy to dry.

Jerusalem artichoke W

Perhaps the easiest winter harvest of all, as long as your digestion can cope (Jerusalem artichokes have a reputation for causing wind). It may be worth cutting the dead stems to just above soil level in December, in case they are blown over by wind, which will dislodge some roots. Use a fork to prise out the clusters of roots whenever needed, searching thoroughly for all the tubers you can find, as they re-grow so willingly. It is worth washing them immediately because the knobby tubers are much easier to clean when freshly harvested.

Harvest of one Jerusalem artichoke plant in December. There is some slug damage.

Kale W, G

Kale plants are a reliable source of deep green or red leaves in all but the coldest weather. Leaf quality and yield go down in January and February, but should recover in March and April. Keep picking the larger, lower leaves, which may brown on their edges if left unpicked. Then, in April, plants switch into flowering mode and produce much smaller leaves but with tender shoots as well, which want picking before their flower buds open. These shoots can be steamed lightly or eaten raw, but become less tender by about mid-May, at which point you can twist out plants

Kale can be picked of its lower leaves at any stage of winter. Then in early spring it makes smaller leaves and tasty shoots. This variety is 'Westland Winter'.

and chop them up for composting, before they pull too much moisture out of the soil.

Land cress W

Pigeons may cause problems as they really like land cress. Keeping them off with netting or fleece is worthwhile because new leaves appear in any milder weather throughout winter and may be quite abundant in March and April. Beautiful yellow flowers in late April and May are also edible.

Leaf beet W, G

As for chard (see page 160), except that leaf beet is more productive and frost hardy.

Leek W, G

As long as you grow varieties of leeks that are fully frost hardy, harvests can be taken at any time until early May. Plants can be repeatedly thinned – removing the larger leeks allows small ones to grow some more. Pull gently on stems and slip a knife into the soil to cut roots off, disturbing the soil as little as possible. You may need a trowel to dig around the stems and help loosen the roots in heavier soil. By May a few flowering stems will be appearing (which are also edible) and, although leeks can still be eaten at that stage, they are less tender and rarely good to eat after the middle of May.

In winters of deep frost, leeks can be harvested frozen and kept in a shed or indoors until needed. A sharp spade is needed, to cut through frozen soil and then under leek roots.

Lettuce W, G

Small lettuces resist frost well, but like so many salad plants they need some protection, mainly from rain and snow, if winter harvests are expected. I find a cloche offers sufficient shelter, and it should be set up to allow some movement of air around the lettuces. Plants can either be kept small by regular picking of their outer leaves, or left to heart up in May. In the former case, harvests can start in February indoors, or early April outdoors, and continue until late June on a weekly basis, with the same plants giving several leaves at a time and reaching nine months of age by the time they flower.

Pulling a leek, variety 'Toledo', which has survived a long spell of cold weather. The soil was reasonably soft under the snow.

Onions just pulled, in early August, from a dug bed in front and an undug bed behind.

Onion (bulb) & shallot S

Onions and shallots need to be dry and disease free if they are to keep all winter – see page 87 for advice on mildew. Bulbs can be lifted, by pulling and with a trowel underneath, when some of their necks are starting to fall over. It may be tempting to leave them to grow more, but I have found that best-quality bulbs come from removing them, on average, in July for shallots and during the first week of August for onions. Then, if they can be laid out somewhere under cover to dry, so much the better; the ground they were occupying can be sown with turnips straight away, or planted with winter salads such as endive or chicory. Alternatively, bulbs can be left outside where they grew, ideally in some dry sunshine, for at least a week after being pulled, until leaves are more brown than green, before being brought inside.

Onion, salad G

The beauty of growing your own salad (spring) onions is being able to pick them at the size you most enjoy, from pencil-thin in April to thick-stemmed, white-bulbed onions in May and June. When they are growing in clumps or a thickly sown row, use a sharp knife to cut out the thickest ones and leave their smaller neighbours to grow some more, for harvesting over at least a month – all from one late-summer sowing.

Oriental leaves W, G

The hardiest oriental leaf is 'Green in the Snow' mustard; it is also extremely pungent. Most others can survive a winter that is not too cold, especially when covered in fleece to protect them from wind; then they should manage some worthwhile growth in March and April, and some nice flower stems from early April to early May. Tatsoi is often the first to flower, followed by pak choi, komatsuna, mizuna, leaf radish and the mustards.

Picking 'Green in the Snow' mustard in November; leaves are slightly holed by heat-seeking slugs!

Parsley W, G

Both curly and flat-leaved parsley are able to survive a lot of winter weather, but go semi-dormant in January and February, before some new leaves herald the arrival of early spring. Flat-leaved parsley subsequently starts flowering in April, and curled parsley flowers in May: both can be kept going a little longer by pinching out all flowering stems, but leaves become smaller as plants are putting their energy into making seed. It is really worth bringing a couple of large parsley plants, in a 22-25cm (9-10") pot, indoors to a windowsill for winter: a surprising amount of new leaves grow, and they are nutritious in salad, containing lots of vitamin C.

Digging out 'White Gem' parsnips in January frost; the ground was kept less frozen by snow.

Parsnip W

A well-grown row or bed of parsnips is most reassuring when winter turns icy. Parsnips have an amazing ability to survive low temperatures, and the issue is more how to dig them out in deep frost. Laying some straw, hay or anything fibrous on top will help keep the soil less frozen, although I find that surface-composted clay keeps soft enough at depth for roots to be available in temperatures as low as -10°C (14°F). Use a fork or spade to lever parsnips out; if they are long it may not be possible to extract the whole root, but sometimes you will find that a 60cm (2') long root emerges, showing the incredible ability of parsnips to forage at depth for moisture and nutrients. By late winter there will be new growth emerging from roots, and when this turns into a flower stem in late April, roots become woody.

Parsnips can also be harvested in early winter, to store – see page 184.

Pea shoots G

Peas sown indoors in January and February, or outdoors in March and April, give some delicious early salad in the hungry gap. Indoor sowings can be in small pots or modules, three seeds in each, planted out when peas are 5-7cm (2-3") high. Space clumps of seedlings, or sow direct with three seeds per hole, at 25-30cm (10-12").

Even though pea plants are frost hardy, all sowings and plantings will benefit from a cover of fleece or a cloche until ready for a first harvest, both to provide warmth and to keep birds off. Wait until plants are 20-30cm (8-12") high, then pinch out 5cm (2") from the top to eat. New shoots then appear from the lower stem, which also continues growing upwards, and new stems appear from the soil, for harvests every week or so over the next two months.

By June there will be flowers turning into pods, edible at all stages until pods become stringy, depending on the variety used. If you stop picking at this stage, allowing pods to fill with peas, there will be a smaller harvest than if no shoots had been picked previously.

Potato S

Keep a close eye out for blight on leaves of potatoes from late June onwards, and cut stems off immediately if you see any leaves turning a mushy brown, to prevent blight spores from passing down into the tubers, which can be harvested then or later. In dry weather when blight is absent, wait for leaves to be about half yellow before pulling stems to extract most of the potatoes, then use a trowel or fork to hunt carefully for any others. If the weather is dry and sunny, tubers can be left on top of the soil for a day or two to dry out their skins: this enables them to keep better when sacked up. Harvesting of non-blighted second earlies is usually in August; maincrop in September.

Rhubarb G

Early varieties such as 'Timperley Early' can produce small leaves by the end of February and be in full flow by early April. Twist off the first leaves when their stems are only 15-20cm (6-8") long; this makes way for more leaves to grow, with longer stems, as spring unfolds. By May and June you may well have more rhubarb than you can eat, and it makes a great gift for hungry neighbours.

Rocket (salad & wild) W, G

Rocket plants of both types keep offering outdoor leaves until the first hard frosts, then go dormant. If frosts are only slight, salad rocket may grow all the time, but slowly in midwinter. By March there can be some healthy new growth, then in April there will be flower stems as well, which are tasty and spicy.

Wild rocket comes into its own from April to early June, with an abundance of small, peppery leaves that can either be picked in bunches or cut at two- to three-week intervals.

Seakale G

Seakale is usually recommended for forcing, but it tastes delicious as a cooked green leaf vegetable as well. Twist or cut medium-sized leaves, which should appear some time in April, or earlier after a mild winter. To force some tender shoots, place an upturned pot over one or more plants in March and, within two or three weeks, if not too cold, there should be some long and tasty stems.

Using an upturned pot to blanch seakale in April. The plant is weakened but the stems are sweet.

Sorrel W, G

Sorrel deserves to be more widely grown. Once you have a clump or two, small harvests of salad are possible from early March. As with parsley, sorrel can be potted up and kept

Picking a leaf of broad-leaved sorrel for salad, with some stem, which is also good to eat.

on a windowsill, giving small pickings through much of the winter. Outdoors, growth by April becomes vigorous and larger leaves are excellent for use in omelettes. By May there are flower stems among the leaves: if these are removed a few times, over two or three weeks, the plant should go back into growing mainly leaves after June, especially when its roots are kept moist.

Spinach W, G

Spinach is a reliable cropper in spring. In the hard winter of 2009/10 I sowed some 'Early Prickly' spinach on 30 August, directly in a bed after carrots were harvested. It was regularly nibbled by slugs through the autumn and leaves were of medium size by winter. Three months of frost and snow left me wondering if they would survive, but almost every plant came through, and gave tasty new leaves for salad by the end of March. Prior to that I cleared off some older, yellowing leaves to compost, and removed a few slugs in the process. Overwintered spinach should crop heavily in April and until flowering in the second half of May, by which time you can have leaves on spinach sown in March.

Even by late September these 'Orange Hokkaido' squash are almost hard and dry.

Squash, winter S

Fruits of squash, to store through winter, should not be harvested too early. It is best to wait until early autumn when most of the leaves have died – a sign that squashes have matured to the point of having hard, dry skins. They are most easily harvested by cutting through the plant's stem on both sides of their stalks, which are often too hard to get a knife through. Be careful, because squashes won't keep if their stalks break away from the main body of fruit. As regards frost, they can tolerate slight, brief autumn frosts of -2 or -3°C (28-27°F), but no lower. In Somerset I harvest them through October, and if there are any with slightly green stalks I bring them indoors to finish drying.

This 'Medania' spinach survived the cold of December 2010, with its leaf quality little affected by freezing.

crop and store them; otherwise they can stay in the soil until needed, perhaps earthed up. The first new leaves of roots in March and April are tasty in salads.

Winter purslane W

This is an extremely hardy plant, but its leaves lose colour in freezing weather. From about late March it starts to flower, and its first flowers and stems are delicious to eat, as well as being pretty. Protecting with fleece or a cloche increases harvests a lot: winter purslane indoors can be the most productive leaf of all, when cut carefully. I trim its outer leaves, and never run a knife horizontally across the top of plants. Imagine a pastry cutter descending around the plant, leaving its central crown intact, which after another week becomes a bountiful clump again. Plants are best removed by late April, because after flowering each one can scatter hundreds of tiny seeds.

Swede W

A few nicely developed swedes are a joyful sight in the autumn, because they are so easy to leave alone and then harvest when needed. Mostly they keep well *in situ*, whatever the weather, and if pigeons eat their leaves in winter it does not affect the roots, which have finished growing. To harvest, push them to one side and run a knife underneath the other side at a slight angle, to cut off roots and soil. By April, any remaining roots will start to shoot again, and then become rather woody.

Turnip & winter radish S, W

These roots are hardy, but less so than swedes. If expecting frosts of more than about -7°C (19°F), it may be wise to harvest your whole

'Helenor' swede harvested on a cold January day, by pulling gently and cutting through the roots.

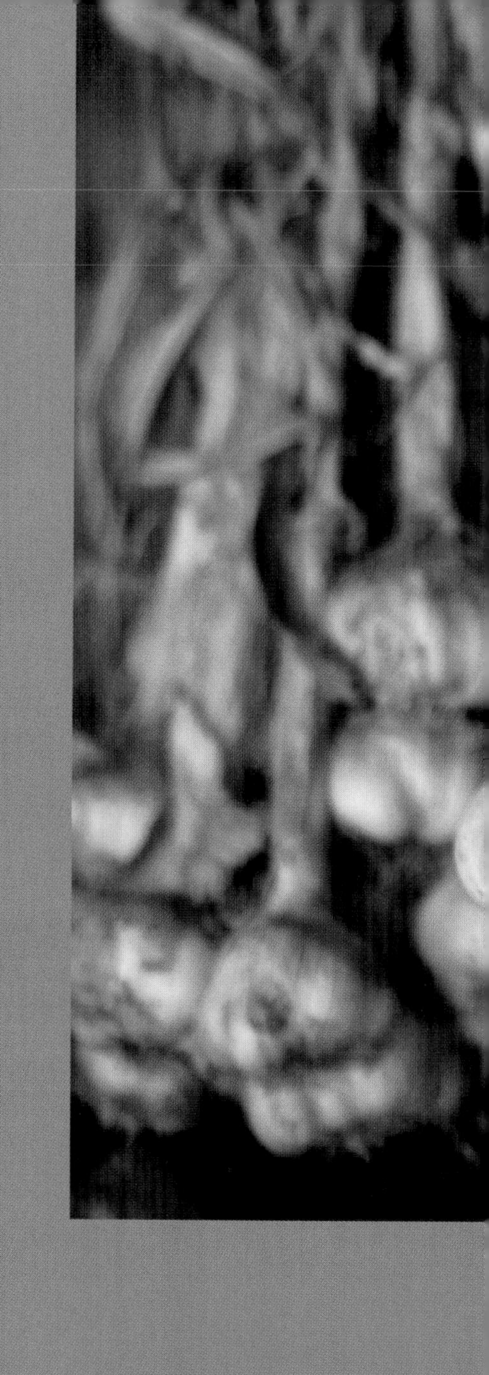

PART 5

Stored harvests

Chapter 12

Principles of storing for winter

It's all about moisture and temperature

Many winter vegetables can be kept for a long time. Squashes, onions and celeriac even keep their looks, but most vegetables tend to become less attractive in store. Be reassured, however, that they still taste good: slightly wilted roots, for example, often have more concentrated flavours than fresh ones.

Most vegetables keep best when cool & slightly damp

Most root vegetables, as well as leeks and hearted cabbage, are biennial plants, dormant through winter while waiting to grow again in any warmth. So for best eating quality they need to be kept as cold as possible, just above freezing, so that they remain in a dormant state.

If temperatures are higher than ideal, say 10°C (50°F) for several weeks, they lose quality and start to re-grow. Any new leaves coming out of roots, for example, are taking goodness and moisture away from the bit we want to eat.

Leafy vegetables keep best in the cold and damp for a different reason: they are less

Biennial vegetables

'Biennial' means that plants do their growing in a year or part of a year before winter, at which time they stop growing while changes in temperature and daylight trigger them into flowering when spring arrives. Many biennial vegetables have been bred to grow large roots of good flavour.

Of the vegetables detailed here, only leeks and salad plants actually grow more after winter, although quite briefly, before flowering in May.

Right: 'Orange Hokkaido', 'Small Kabocha', 'Tonda Padana', 'Buttercup' and 'Hungarian Blue' squashes.

6kg (13lb) of onions from a 3m (10') row were pulled two weeks earlier and dried in the sun.

likely to wilt. I have included salad leaves in this section because it is useful to know how they may best be kept for a week at a time – saving you from having to go out and pick them too often in winter.

As regards frost, a few stored vegetables can resist it and most others cannot. Potato tubers are especially susceptible to frost damage.

Some exceptions to cool & damp

Onions, garlic and winter squash keep best in warm and dry conditions. They are wrapped in a dry skin, their own home-made packaging, and keeping this skin dry helps to steer them away from thoughts of re-growing. Leaving them out in fine weather for a week or so after harvest is a good start to long-term storage; if squash are harvested too late for warm sun, they benefit from being kept in a warm, dry place for a week or more after harvest, to harden and dry out their skins.

Garlic and onions can be stored in low temperatures, even below freezing, as long as the air is dry. Potatoes keep best when dry, but go mushy if frozen.

Where to store

Few of us have the facilities for keeping harvests in the absolute optimum state, so we need to make best use of any spaces we have.

For vegetables needing to be kept cool, an outdoor shed or garage is suitable. For instance, roots can be kept in sacks and covered with a rug or blanket in frosty weather. However, rats and mice will appreciate such a cosy larder in which to live: my barn has a few rat runs and I put some poison in them each autumn, when rats are coming indoors.

Leafy vegetables need their moisture conserving as well as being cool: for example, salad hearts and leaves are best kept in polythene bags, as cool as possible without freezing, either in a fridge or a cool place outdoors.

Onions and garlic do not dry out, so they can be hung up in ropes or bunches, under cover outside or in drier, indoor conditions for longer storage.

Long-term storage of root vegetables

Biennial root vegetables can be stored for many months. They include beetroot, carrots, celeriac, garlic, onions, potatoes and turnips. Parsnips and swedes can also be kept a long time indoors, but survive more healthily in the soil they grew in.

It is also possible to store larger quantities of vegetables in outdoor 'clamps', by piling them up on straw-covered soil, then covering with straw, cardboard and soil to keep frost out.

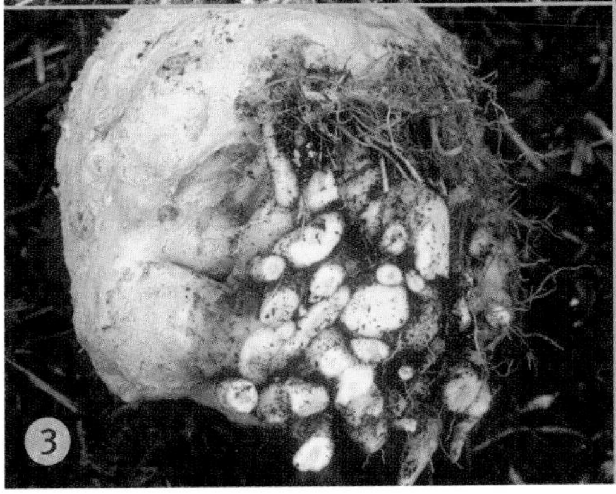

Celeriac harvested

1. When celeriac is pulled out of the soil, you can see its multitude of mostly superficial roots.
2. Most of these roots are being cut off and all the leaves have been removed.
3. The main root now has its smaller roots sufficiently trimmed for long-term storage, with some soil to retain moisture.

This method was used when people had no recourse to bought food and needed a large supply of winter food, for themselves as well as their animals. For most of us now, indoor storage of roots in sacks is more practical.

Roots can also be stored in boxes with damp sand or moist compost around them – this is more work than simply putting them in a sack, but should keep them in better condition, as long as the box is cool.

The ultimate long-term store

Leaving roots in the soil is a magnificent way of preserving their freshness and flavour. Parsnips, swedes and Jerusalem artichokes keep well like this, without protection, but other roots need some help. In Britain the two main ones are beetroot and celeriac, which can be fleeced in November to keep them from freezing too hard. They tolerate some frost, just not too much, and two or three layers of fleece is worthwhile if you want to leave them outside, until they start to grow again in April.

These 'Cheltenham Green Top' beetroot were covered with fleece before really cold weather arrived, helping them survive -12°C (10°F).

Carrots can also be left in the ground but need something fibrous on top, such as straw, or newspaper with some mesh over it, to keep frost out. However, slugs enjoy this mulched environment and some damage is likely.

Short-term storage

Occasional harvests of outdoor leafy vegetables, such as Brussels sprouts, savoy cabbage, kale and salad leaves, can be stored for a week or two so that trips to the plot are reduced, especially in difficult weather. They keep best in polythene bags at low temperatures, just above freezing.

Sorting root vegetables at harvest time

The only vegetables that will keep in good condition for many months are those that are of best quality to start with. All roots, hearts (and fruits) with any defects should be kept aside for immediate use, or stored separately for using before the best of your harvest.

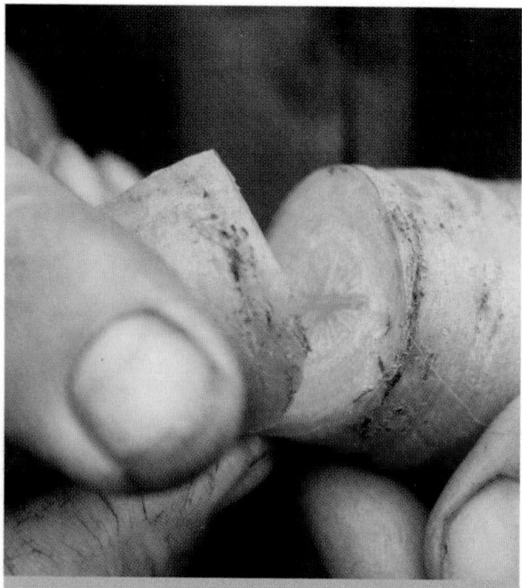

This carrot reveals the small white maggot of carrot root fly and the brown damage it caused.

Checking stored vegetables in midwinter

* After about two months of storage it is worth tipping out the remaining roots in sacks, or looking through vegetables in boxes, to sort out any that are decaying and may infect others with fungal moulds. Even when harvested carefully, there are nearly always a few vegetables that do not keep well.

Any roots with noticeable amounts of insect damage, especially carrots, should be kept for eating as soon as possible, partly because they are more likely to rot at some point, and partly because, in the case of carrot fly larvae, the larvae continue eating all winter.

All roots with even tiny spots of fungal rotting, such as blight on potatoes and black spots on carrots and beetroot, also need eating rather than keeping. Smaller roots are best set aside for early use, because large ones keep better. A little soil should be left on roots to protect their skins and retain some moisture.

Sacks for storing root vegetables

Old potato or grain sacks serve well, of two-ply or preferably three-ply paper. Hessian sacks can be expensive and are inclined to rot when damp for a long period. Paper sacks retain a reasonable amount of moisture and breathe enough to discourage fungal rotting.

Freezing, dehydrating & sterilising

This is a brief mention for summer harvests, whose excess can be conserved in different ways to add some variety to winter fare.

Cleaning stored root vegetables for the table

* After more than about two weeks in store, the soil on roots becomes hard and more difficult to brush off before preparing them to eat. It works well to rub off larger soil lumps first, then soak roots in water for half an hour or so, to soften the remaining soil before brushing roots clean.

Freezing is possible for beans, peas, tomatoes, broccoli and courgettes, although I find that peas and broad beans keep their quality and flavour better than other vegetables when frozen. To freeze these vegetables, blanch briefly in boiling water and then seal them with minimal air in polythene bags. Tomatoes conserve well when boiled up, allowed to cool and the puree frozen in plastic pots. Eating these vegetables is a tantalising reminder of the tastes of summer.

Dehydrating works well if you have or can borrow a machine. Warm air is blown gently over thin strips (0.6cm or ¼") of almost any vegetable and fruit, until nearly all the moisture is gone, taking 18-24 hours. Then the leathery strips can be packed in jars for keeping at room temperature, and have a better flavour than many frozen vegetables. I have done this with tomatoes, sweet peppers, cucumbers, beetroot, carrots, apples, pears and stinging nettle tops.

Sterilising – boiling in sealed jars to sterilise and pasteurise – is good for certain summer vegetables. French beans should be blanched for two minutes, then packed into jars and covered with slightly salted water. Tomatoes, courgettes, aubergines and peppers need cooking lightly to soften them, before being spooned into jars. Jars should have their lids sealed tight and then be covered with water in a pan on heat; this water should boil for around an hour. When it has cooled, the jars can be removed and kept for at least a year if need be.

These 'Karmazyn' broad beans have been shelled and are ready for blanching briefly in boiling water before freezing.

Chapter 13

Vegetables for winter storage A–Z

Keeping vegetables alive after harvest

In just three words, successful storage means *keeping vegetables alive*. This involves slightly different methods and conditions for each kind of vegetable, as listed in the table on page 180 and in the A–Z. I have included here the main vegetables that grow well in a maritime Atlantic climate such as Britain's and can be kept for shorter or longer periods during the winter season.

Once harvested, most vegetables keep best in cool and moist conditions. But it is worth knowing the exceptions, such as squash, onions and garlic. These store best in dry, warm air indoors or, in the case of onions and garlic, really cool dry air outdoors.

One obstacle to successful storage may be rats, and if they are suspected or noticed, it is worth putting a sachet of poison near to stored roots and replacing it with another if it disappears, and so on until the rats are poisoned.

Temperature levels from December to March can vary considerably, which makes a huge difference to the quality of stored produce. Cold winters mean that root vegetables such as potatoes and carrots will stay firm and fresh in a frost-free shed or outbuilding.

A balance of stored & growing harvests

This temperature variation is another reason for having some vegetables in store, as a reserve for extreme weather when outdoor vegetables are not growing and may even be damaged. If, on the other hand, it is a mild winter, the stored produce will keep less well, but there will be better harvests of outdoor vegetables such as leeks, kale, lamb's lettuce and purple sprouting broccoli. Also, the harvests of hungry gap vegetables such as spring cabbage will start earlier.

Right: Onions as dry as these should keep well until April.

Requirements for best storage of each vegetable				
Vegetable & month of harvests for storage	Maximum storage time*	Temp. guide (°C)**	Humid? 1 = dry, 5 = damp	Or leave where grown
Beans, dried: Sept-Oct	2 years	Any	1	No
Beetroot: Nov-Dec	4-5 months	0-10	3	Possibly
Brussels sprouts: Oct-Apr	2 weeks	0-5	5	Yes
Cabbage, ballhead: Oct-Dec	4-5 months, until Apr	1-10	4	Some varieties
Cabbage, savoy: Oct-Apr	2 weeks	0-5	5	Yes
Carrot: Oct-Nov	4-5 months, until Apr	1-10	3	If mulched
Celeriac: Nov-Dec	Nov-Apr	0-10	3	Possibly
Chicory heart: Nov-Dec	6-8 weeks	1-5	5	No
Chinese cabbage: Nov	6 weeks	1-5	5	No
Endive heart: Oct-Dec	3 weeks	1-5	5	No
Garlic: July	July-May	Below 5, above 15	1	No
Jerusalem artichoke: Oct-Apr	4 weeks	0-10	4	Yes
Kale: Oct-May	1 week	0-5	5	Yes
Leek: Oct-Apr	4-6 weeks	1-10	5	Yes
Onion/shallot: July-Aug	9-10 months	Below 5, above 15	1	No
Parsnip: Oct-Apr	Nov-Apr	0-10	3	Yes
Potato: Aug-Sept	Aug-Apr	1-10	2	No
Salad leaves	1 week	2-7	5	Yes
Squash, winter: Oct	Oct-Apr	16-20	1	No
Swede: Oct-Apr	Oct-Apr	1-10	3	Yes
Turnip & winter radish: Oct-Apr	3 months	1-10	3	Possibly

* Vegetables keep longest, and in best condition, at the lower temperatures.
** Root vegetables store in top condition at 1-2°C (34-36°F). (NB 1°C = 1.8°F +32)

Beetroot

Beetroot is relatively easy to store when roots are larger than tennis-ball sized, which helps them to keep moist and firm. The harvest date can be as late as you dare, before any frost of about -4°C (25°F). In really mild winters or locations, beetroot may stand outdoors, and soil can be pulled up around roots for protection, but mostly it is safer to bring them indoors. Leave a little soil on the roots and then put them in a paper or hessian sack.

A storage temperature of around 5°C (41°F) should see roots keeping until March or even April, by which time they will be growing some quite long, thin leaves. Moving roots into light at this point (or earlier), in a pot of

Three large beetroot in a pot of compost growing salad leaves indoors in February.

compost, will provide some early salad leaves. In fact, if you have a giant root it may give better value as a 'leaf generator' over winter, in a pot of compost – see picture above.

Brussels sprouts

These store in good condition for a week or so after harvest, if kept as cool as possible without freezing. Brussels sprouts kept for more than a week will start to yellow, so extra trimming of their outer leaves is then necessary before eating them.

Cabbage, winter

Dense hearts of red and white ballhead cabbage can be picked with two or three outer leaves left on, in November or even December before frosts of -3°C (27°F) or more. Pack them in a box or crate, lined with polythene but open on top, then keep them as cool as possible, down to 1°C (34°F), and they will stay in fair condition until April. At a higher temperature, some deterioration of outer leaves will happen over a few weeks. They won't look good but loss of quality is only external: rotting and withered outside leaves can be peeled off to reveal the good heart inside.

All savoys, including crinkly-hearted cabbages such as 'Tundra' and 'January King', can be harvested fresh, or kept below 10°C (50°F) for a week or two between harvest and eating.

Carrot

There are two choices for storing carrots. Roots harvested in late October to November, placed in paper or hessian sacks without cleaning the roots, then kept at temperatures below 10°C (50°F), should store until April if not eaten before. By then they will have quite long shoots of new leaves, which need snapping off before cleaning them to eat. There may also be some annoyingly large tunnels made by carrot root flies, which chomp away all winter, whether carrots are in the soil or in sacks.

In free-draining soil carrots can be stored in the ground (see Chapter 11, page 159).

Celeriac

Large celeriac are probably the easiest of vegetables to store, as they have plenty of dry matter and barely shrivel, nor do they go soft from growing new leaves. Harvest in November or December, and leave some soil around all the small roots. Keep them in a box, crate or sack, below 10°C (50°F), and they should keep in a fair state until April. Celeriac can be harvested frozen and thawed indoors.

Chicory hearts

These keep in good condition for six to eight weeks in a household fridge, inside polythene bags to retain moisture. In the (usually) slightly higher temperatures of a shed or garage, they can be kept for up to a month, or longer if cold. Some outer leaves decay all the time and need peeling off before use, while a few hearts may rot for no apparent reason. It is worth trying to store some through Christmas and into January, because there are so few other salad leaves at that time, and the colour of red chicories is most uplifting in midwinter.

Chinese cabbage

Treat Chinese cabbage similarly to chicory hearts (above), but keep them cold: any temperatures above 5°C (41°F) will soon result in some unpleasant-smelling outer leaves. Large, tight hearts keep best.

Endive hearts

These are the most difficult hearts of all to store because their open habit allows moisture to escape, yet keeping them moist in polythene bags can lead to browning of leaf tips from fungal infections, unless they are really cool. If you have space in the fridge, they are worth a try. Or dig up the plant with a tennis-ball-sized clump of roots and soil, wrap the latter in polythene and keep at 0-10°C (32-50°F) for up to three weeks.

Garlic

Wonderful garlic, harvested before summer has barely begun, is one of the easiest vegetables to keep in good condition until the following spring. The secret is to harvest at a good moment, in late June or early July, while bulbs are a tiny bit immature and have plenty of skin layers around their cloves. Leave them outside to dry for a week or so, then bring into an airy place, out of full sunlight, where they can be laid out on a bench to dry a little, before either plaiting or simply bunching them. Plaits or bunches keep best in a warm and dry atmosphere; cold and dry is also

This heart of Chinese cabbage survived frost because it is still loose-leaved and green, rather than firm.

Kale survives most frost and snow. This 'Westland Winter' suffered more from pigeons.

'Autumn Mammoth Goliath' leeks survive moderate frost but may suffer in severe conditions.

good, but cold usually means more damp, which can encourage some rotting of bulbs from the root end (a few always go soft). Most should keep until they start sprouting in April, or May indoors – still edible and with a more pungent flavour.

Kale

Kale is best picked fresh, but it does keep well for up to a week in a polythene bag, as cool as possible. In frosty weather, kale can be picked frozen and thawed out indoors.

Jerusalem artichoke

Although tubers keep well in the soil, they can also be dug and stored as for beetroot (see page 180), as cool and damp as possible. This gives peace of mind if your garden soil is clay, when there is the possibility of slugs eating a few roots.

Leek

Leeks are normally pulled when needed, as long as the soil is not frozen solid. If such weather is forecast, and even if the leeks themselves are frozen, a month's supply (or more) can be pulled, left untrimmed with their roots and some soil on, and placed in a box, crate, bucket or carrier bag. Keep them in a cool but mostly frost-free shed or garage and then, when needed, they can be trimmed as usual.

Onion

Like garlic, onion stores well in dry conditions, as long as mildew has not infected the bulbs (see page 87). Leave bulbs to dry outside for a week or two, as long as you have space and the weather is mainly dry. Then they can be laid out in shallow boxes, which could be stacked, or tie them in bunches or

Onions store well unless infected with downy mildew, not always obvious from the outside.

These 'Gladiator' parsnips will keep better for being covered in soil, preferably in a sack.

plaits to hang somewhere with movement of air. Best storage is achieved by leaving the dry stems on until close to the time of use. Mildew is difficult because it causes onions to rot internally, while they still look all right from the outside.

Sometimes an invisible infection of mildew reveals itself only after several weeks or even months, as a softening around the neck, which when cut through reveals grey, rotten onion. This should be burned, not composted. If no mildew is present, onions should keep until they shoot in spring. The increasing prevalence of mildew is turning a previously easy vegetable into something quite difficult.

Parsnip

Medium to large parsnips keep well after harvest, for the whole winter if needed, but shrivel a little and taste less sweet than roots left in soil, which are exposed to more frost. Keep harvested parsnips cool and with some soil on, in paper sacks. In early April, I recommend digging all remaining roots to keep in a cool shed, which will then be less warm than the soil, and you could still be eating parsnips in early May.

Potato

Potatoes need low, frost-free temperatures to keep well, otherwise they start to grow again, with long, white, fleshy shoots which take goodness and moisture out of tubers; these shoots can be rubbed off before cooking. Aim for tubers to be as dry as possible when you put them in paper or hessian sacks, then keep the sacks in your coolest spot. Keep an eye out for dark, damp spots on the outside of sacks, which almost certainly indicate a well-rotten tuber infected by blight: at the first sign of this, tip out all the potatoes and remove any slimy, decaying tubers. Those next to them, which may well be wet, can still be eaten if they have not started to rot inside.

Salad leaves

After harvesting your leaves, at any time of year, give them a rinse in cold water and drain in a colander. Any that are not to be eaten straight away can be bagged up, with some moisture on, in polythene bags that will fit in a fridge: or, in winter, in a cool but frost-free space outdoors. They should keep in good condition for a week or more and it saves a lot of time to have some always ready for eating.

Squash, winter

Squash is the best vegetable to store indoors, and they look nice in a sitting room if there is enough space, perhaps on a windowsill or on top of a dresser. When harvested with hard, dry skins, squash should keep until April. Any mouldiness normally begins around their stems with a rapidly spreading soft, grey spot: eat them quickly if you see this.

'Manchester Market' turnips in October, suitable for harvesting to store for two or three months.

Swede

Similar to parsnips, swedes keep best outside and are a nice adornment for the winter garden. They can be stored for a few months indoors as well, in a sack or box, cool and slightly damp.

Turnip & winter radish

Because most varieties of turnip and radish risk being damaged by frosts of about -7°C (19°F), there comes a point when it is worth bringing them in before severe weather arrives. Leave a little soil on them and stack in a box, or place in a sack and keep similarly to beetroot (see page 180). After March the roots grow pale leaves, which are tasty in salads.

These swede leaves were stripped by pigeons in December. While the roots could have been harvested to store at this point, they actually kept well outside until early April.

PART 6

Winter vegetables under cover

Chapter **14**

Under-cover growing

Making the most of wintry weather and low light

Winter in British latitudes offers small opportunities for healthy growth, with poor light levels, so plants have few chances to heal and regenerate. The advantage of cloches, polytunnels and glasshouses is that they protect plants from the many traumas of winter weather, such as wind, rain and continual damp. Even fleece can make a huge difference. However, *these covers do not keep frost out.*

I have noticed, when showing people my winter salads in polytunnels, that they assume the tunnels' plastic is able to conserve enough warmth to protect plants from freezing. This is most certainly not the case, especially between December and early February, when nights are so long that any small solar gain during daylight is almost entirely dissipated by dawn.

Timings and methods for growing many vegetables under cover are described in the next chapter; this chapter looks at materials and structures that enable survival and growth through winter, and also at containers that can be used for indoor growing. It finishes with advice on soil and plant care in winter so that plants burst back into productive life as soon as days lengthen and the temperature rises.

Surviving the winter

From my observations over many winters, I have come to appreciate that winter vegetables, especially salads, have less problem with low temperatures than they do with wind and wet. In 2009/10 I lost almost all *outdoor*, unprotected salads except for lamb's lettuce (corn salad), but the survival rate in a cold polytunnel, where night temperatures fell below -10°C (14°F) on a few occasions, was close to 100 per cent. Just a few lettuces succumbed to fungal rot in their stems – arising from dampness as much as cold.

In the same winter, and also in the cold winter of 2010/11, a simple and home-made cloche, whose sides did not even meet the ground in places, enabled 90-per-cent survival of its salad plants. So did a sheet of fleece that was simply folded double and laid on top of some plants.

Right: These salad plants are happy in the greenhouse, although they were frozen just the night before.

New growth in winter

Survival is one thing; making new growth in winter at a latitude of more than 50 degrees is quite another. It is certainly possible, although growth will be meagre in the darkest two months. The trick is to have sown plants at a time that enables them to establish a root system without growing too large. Then they are able to survive the worst of winter, often growing their roots even more in milder moments, before bouncing back into life after the middle of February, when light and some milder temperatures return.

Suitable covers & structures

Winter covers need to:

- **emphasise the positives** – warmth, light, relative dryness, calm air
- **reduce the negatives** – wind, rain, low temperatures.

There are quite simple and economical ways of achieving some of these aims, enough to make a worthwhile difference. You don't have to spend lots of money on a double-glazed greenhouse with artificial light! The table below will help you assess the advantages and disadvantages of different winter covers for plants. The 'time' column refers to looking after protected plants. Note that 'conservatory' can also mean a windowsill, but the extra light in a large structure is most helpful: on windowsills plants have a tendency to become leggy.

Brushwood and netting

It seems almost bizarre that twigs and thin nets can be effective at protecting plants, which shows the importance of reducing wind, and perhaps they even provide a little extra warmth around leaves. For example, Eliot Coleman in Maine, USA, has found that spinach survived better when small wooden branches with twigs on, rather like pea sticks, were laid on top of plants (*The Winter Harvest Handbook*, see Resources).

Here in Somerset I saw that plants of sprouting broccoli survived a cold winter better when simply covered with a net against pigeons, compared with some of the same plants that had not been netted. The netting was thin and barely visible, with 1cm (½") squares, yet was enough to make a really worthwhile difference. It can be either draped on top of plants, or supported by cloche hoops, or by wooden stakes with upside-down plastic pots on their tops.

Winter covers for plants

	Cost	Time	Light	Water	Ventilate	Output
Net, brushwood	Low	Low	Good	No	No	Low
Fleece	Low	Low	Med	No	No	Low/med
Cloche	Low/med	Low/med	Good	Med	Little	Med
Cold frame	Med/high	Med	Med/good	Med	Med	Med
Polytunnel	Med	High	Good	Med/high	Yes	High
Greenhouse	High	High	Excellent	Med/high	Yes	High
Conservatory	n/a	High	Med/good	Med	Little	Med

Small branches of hazel laid over spinach. These plants survived the winter of 2010/11.

The versatility of fleece

- **Fleece in winter** is mostly about keeping plants alive.
- **Fleece in spring** is for encouraging new growth.

Fleece

Fleece is a thin, lightweight, polypropylene cover. Look for a thicker grade, 25-30g/m², because the thinner sheets of 17g/m² are so fragile that massive splits often appear during their first season, making them impossible to reuse. Fleece of the thicker grades should do for several uses; any small splits or holes do not detract from their effectiveness. After use, simply roll the fleece up and keep in a shed until needed again: don't worry if it is dirty; soil on fleece washes out in the first rain when it is relaid. It is best stored hanging from a roof, not on the floor, so that mice cannot nest in it.

Fleece for midwinter use is more effective when doubled up, as insulation against extremes of cold, which also increases its most general benefit of protecting plants from wind. Where laid directly on top of salad plants in the winter of 2009/10, they nearly all survived, compared with unfleeced plants, which nearly all died. Fleece is easy to use simply placed over plants and held down by stones, bricks or pegs every metre (3') or so along all sides, and stretched fairly tight. It can also be used on cloche hoops, but is then more at risk of breaking in a winter gale.

By the end of February, fleece has a different role and is best used in single thickness,

Bed covered in fleece through January and February, to protect from weather and birds.

Removing fleece on 5 March to pick salad. Pigeons would have eaten the land cress.

Another advantage of no-dig

With undug beds and paths, early planting becomes easier, involving less mud and allowing rapid growth in undisturbed soil. Using fleece as well, laid on top of young plants in undug beds, encourages even earlier growth.

which converts the extra daylight into warmth while continuing to protect from wind.

For example, in 2010 I set out small plants of spinach and peas on a day in late February when snow was falling. Young plants in 3cm (1") modules were taken straight from an unheated greenhouse and set in the cold soil, then covered with fleece directly on top of them, held down by stones along its sides and ends. Leaves under the fleece were regularly frozen until mid-March, and only slightly thereafter, but they were sufficiently protected and encouraged that almost every plant survived, and by late March there was significant new growth pushing the cover upwards, for harvests of spinach and pea shoots in April.

Cloched salads in December ready for winter – mustard, rocket, endive and lettuce.

Cloches

Home-made cloches work really well and are much cheaper than bought cloches.

Before the advent of cheaper polythene, glass cloches were used to great effect: for example, to grow fully hearted lettuce by April, from plantings in late October. If you can afford glass cloches, they bring even more benefits than the plastic ones described here, but they are also heavier to handle and more difficult to store when not in use. Cloches made of rigid PVC plastic, which behave like glass and are easier to handle, are still expensive.

Hoops for polythene cloches can be made from:

- 18-25mm (¾-1") plastic water pipe
- 12mm (½") plastic electrical conduit
- 3-4mm wire (4mm is best for 1.2m/4' beds).

These all need to be cut so that a slightly flattened, semicircular frame is created over the bed or rows to be covered. Hoops of plastic pipe can be pushed into the soil if it is soft enough, or on to lengths of bamboo.

For the cover, the most important thing is that it stays in place in all weathers. Its sides do not always have to meet the ground or be buried under soil to keep wind out – some ventilation is good for plants inside. The two main weather hazards, high wind and heavy snow, are best resisted by thicker polythene (minimum 480 and preferably 600 gauge), of the same grade as used on polytunnels. Don't use builders' polythene, which goes brittle and starts to fragment after just a season's use.

If using wire hoops, they can be bent around a stick, about 15cm (6") from both ends, to make a loop on either side for retaining polypropylene string to hold down the plastic cover. The string is passed under (not through) the loops of wires, held under them by the loop shape, and then under the next diagonally opposite loop on the other side, crossing the polythene each time and holding it tight; when you reach the end, run the string back in the opposite direction so that it criss-crosses the first run. One long length of string does for a whole cloche.

An occasional watering will be needed on light soils – once a month from November to February – but none at this time on heavy soil, then about fortnightly after that (see 'Watering, ventilating' box, page 195).

Cold frames

Cold frames, also called Dutch lights, were used a great deal in large gardens when labour was cheap in relation to the vegetables grown. They need more input than cloches, and if the sides are made of wood there can be lurking slugs. Glass sides are better in that respect but make the structure more fragile.

You can grow the same winter vegetables in cold frames as under cloches. Keep the top secure in extremely windy weather, but it is generally best to allow some air to enter all the time. Water infrequently in winter, except on light soils.

Such a frame is also good for raising plants if you have a sheltered, sunny spot, and a base of pea gravel will help to discourage slugs.

A small plastic cloche over lettuce in early spring. The uncovered plant has grown markedly less.

Vegetables for winter cloches

Cloches set out in October are good for winter salads, spinach and spring onions sown in early September; they can all be sown or planted and left unprotected at first, as long as the cloche is in place before any severe weather. On light soils with fewer slugs, carrots sown in early October can also be covered, for harvesting after the middle of March. Cloches can also be placed over early sowings and plantings from February.

Polytunnels

For the area they cover, polytunnels are considerably better value than greenhouses (see page 195), although they retain less heat and frosts are more likely inside. Their main winter value is in keeping wind and rain off, and in providing higher daytime temperatures whenever there is brightness and sunshine.

The specifications of polytunnel structures and their polythene covers are continually changing, but here are a few basic guidelines:

- Straight sides are worthwhile, so you can grow crops or run staging right to the edge.
- Look for a tall enough structure that you can comfortably stand up in and that has room to grow tall plants.
- Make sure the polythene allows all ultra-violet light through – especially important for winter vegetables.
- Crop support bars, for summer vegetables, are worth paying extra for.

Polythene lasts for five to seven years. It can be provided, at extra cost, with a means of fixing to the frame rather than you having to dig it into a trench, but this necessitates fixing ground-posts more securely, either with anchor plates or concrete.

Doors come in many forms and a hinged door is the easiest to use, but you need room for it

Clearing snow from polytunnels

The weight of deep snow can damage polytunnel hoops if there is insufficient wind to blow it off, so it is occasionally necessary to sweep snow down to the sides with a long broom. Also, this allows light to enter – it is surprisingly dark under snow-covered or even deeply frosted polythene.

Tunnels resist the weight of snow to a certain point but I am nervous at seeing too much on them.

Let all the light in

* It is worth cleaning the plastic every year, with a damp sheet or soft wet brush, mainly outside and also sometimes inside, to remove lichen and moss. These can build up to a surprising degree, enough to impede growth in reduced light.

to swing outwards. Roll-up doors are simple, compact and effective. A wooden frame with netting is useful for keeping birds and cats out when doors are left open.

For more on tunnel structures, see Resources.

Heating a tunnel is not worthwhile, because polythene has such a low insulation value. For best results in winter, grow plants that tolerate being frozen and are able to make new growth in low temperatures – see Chapter 15.

For propagation that requires higher temperatures, a kit with electric cable in sand, controlled by a thermostat, is the most economical way of providing small amounts of consistent warmth. Fleece is also useful inside polytunnels, both on seedlings and on vegetables.

Watering, ventilating

Plants in polytunnels in winter need little watering and regular ventilation. For winter salad plants, I keep a door at both ends *open all the time*, both day and night, because cool air moving gently over plants is better than stagnant air, which leads to mildew on leaves and other fungal problems. From late November to February I water once, soaking the soil and then allowing it to dry out on the surface. This also discourages slugs.

Greenhouses

The extra cost of glass over plastic is balanced by its advantages in extra durability, light admission, ventilation, heat retention and aesthetic quality. Small greenhouses are excellent for propagating hundreds of high-quality plants in a season, which can make a huge difference to the success or otherwise of a vegetable plot.

Through the winter months, a range of salads in soil or on staging, in boxes and pots of any kind (see overleaf), can be harvested in worthwhile amounts over a long period.

Accept the midwinter lull

* Supplying heat to winter vegetables is not worth it, because low light levels mean that plants cannot grow much between mid-November and early February, even when given some extra warmth. And if you supply light as well, a lot of energy is used for relatively small harvests. An extra layer of insulation, such as bubble wrap, is more economical.

My home-made greenhouse is here made foggy for some hours by mild, damp air after cold.

For growing in the soil or in growbags at ground level, you need a greenhouse with glass to ground level. If all growth is to happen on staging, a masonry base is good for conserving warmth at night.

Conservatories

For growing winter salads and herbs especially, indoor spaces such as conservatories and even windowsills are a cheap option, with useful background warmth from the house. The quality of growth depends mainly on how much light is admitted, but even windows facing only one direction can be successful. See 'Container-grown winter salads', right, and Chapter 15 for ideas. Parsley, coriander and chervil are especially useful in the house.

Container-grown winter salads

Salads will grow productively in containers indoors, even in the coldest weather.

Suitable containers

Any container that holds a reasonable amount of compost and has drainage holes in the bottom can serve. I have used and reused all of the following:

- Old plastic mushroom boxes, lined with newspaper (30x40cm/12x15").
- Old polystyrene fish boxes with eight or ten small holes cut in their bottoms.
- Pots of 15-30cm (6-12") in size.
- Seed trays (usually 23x37cm/9x15").

Planting boxes of winter salad

1. Mushroom boxes have been lined with newspaper and are being filled with compost and cow manure, one of each.
2. In the middle of October, plants have been set out, from sowings made in modules a month earlier.
3. Five weeks later there is significant growth and some leaves were picked; most of these plants survived a cold winter (indoors).

Conclusion: all plants grew well. Those in compost survived best, giving leaves until April.

The seed trays were least productive because they hold less compost. Deeper containers give a longer period of harvest as plants are able to keep growing, with greater reserves of moisture and nutrients. Otherwise, some feeding is worthwhile in March and April.

Composts for filling

The best results I ever had were from boxes 10cm (4") deep, filled mostly with well-rotted cow manure and a thin layer of finer compost on top, all pressed in firmly and right to the top. Seedlings were module-sown in late August and planted into this rich material in September, their larger leaves picked off from October onwards, and they finished cropping in late April with no extra feeding.

Most multipurpose composts will run low on nutrients by March, hence the value of well-decomposed manure. One-year-old, home-made compost is also excellent and may contain as many nutrients as manure, depending on your heap's ingredients. Green waste compost is too low on nutrients.

Tips on growing & harvesting

Seed can be sown direct into containers in late August to early September, or plants raised in modules or pots can be put in place by early October. Spacing of plants should be generous, around 10cm (4") for each one.

For example, in a mushroom box that measures 30x37cm (12x15") I grow six or eight plants in two rows of three or four plants each (see photos, left). Giving more space to plants helps them to crop for considerably longer, with leaves of better quality and with less, if any, mildew.

Container-grown salads benefit from regular picking of their larger leaves to keep plants on the small side, maintain leaf health and conserve nutrients. New leaves are small anyway in midwinter, then grow larger and thicker from late February until flowering from about the middle of April.

Watering containers in winter

Containers hold less moisture than soil so they need more frequent watering – approximately fortnightly from late November to late February, then weekly at least after that and more frequently again for small containers.

Mustards 'Green in the Snow', 'Red Frills' and 'Red Giant' (also chicory, right) were sown in September. This is on 2 April after three cuts.

The same box ten minutes later after cutting healthy leaves to eat and removing some yellow ones; there was one more harvest after this.

If leaves start to show paler yellow and purple tinges in late winter, containers need feeding. Follow instructions on proprietary labels but at about half dose in winter and until March, because growth is still slow, then feed at the normal rate in April.

Once plants become more stem than leaf in May, pull them out for composting and spread the container compost on beds or borders.

Tips for best harvests indoors

Every little extra thing you do well is a help to plants that are growing so slowly through winter. The tips offered here are based on my experience of much cool-season growing.

Soil care, sowing & planting

My calendar of indoor growing starts with soil preparation in May, after removal of winter salad plants. I plant a selection of summer vegetables, such as tomatoes and melons, into soil that has been covered in about 5cm (2") of one or other (or a mixture) of:

- composted manure, dark brown and reasonably crumbly
- home-made compost, well rotted; can still be slightly lumpy
- bought compost such as spent mushroom compost

For winter leaves, salad seed should be sown by mid-September, at a time when tomatoes and other summer crops are still growing, which is why it works better to raise plants in modules or pots, for planting as soon as summer vegetables are pulled out.

Then when the summer crops are removed, by mid-October at the latest, salad and winter vegetable plants can be set out. The only soil

Soil preparation & planting
1. May 2010: after clearing winter salad plants that were flowering, 5cm (2") of well-rotted cow manure has been spread on the soil before planting tomatoes, cucumbers, peppers, etc.
2. Preparing soil after removing sweet pepper plants in mid-October: treading down lumps and making it smooth.
3. Mid-October: planting winter salad modules into dibbed holes after watering the soil thoroughly; plants are also watered in.

preparation consists of walking on the beds to tread soil back down and break up any large lumps of compost. I dib holes into the firmed soil for plants raised in modules, and seed can also be sown direct: carrots in early October, for example. There is enough residual fertility for winter vegetables without adding any extra compost or feeding in any way.

Watering indoor soil in winter

Winter growth is slow and requires much less water than in summer. Start off by giving soil a thorough soak after summer crops are removed, to replace the moisture they have pulled out, often to a considerable depth. I aim to really saturate the soil before planting or sowing winter vegetables. Check with a trowel that water has soaked in – you may find it still dry underneath and in need of more watering.

Then it is possible to water infrequently, monthly on free-draining soil; less on heavy soil in midwinter. Make sure the soil is fully moistened every time, then between each watering it will gradually dry out on top, helping to keep slug numbers down and keep mildew at bay. During March the tempo increases, to watering fortnightly, and then weekly by April, or earlier if the weather is sunny.

It is good to water thoroughly in October, to be sure that soil is fully moist before winter.

Dealing with slugs indoors

There are many fewer pests in winter than in summer, but slugs endure. Slow plant growth means that even small amounts of slug nibbling can cause significant damage, especially at sowing and planting time. Slugs are drawn to recently sown and planted vegetables, so be vigilant in September and October. I keep a sharp knife to hand for cutting them by torchlight, mainly straight after planting.

During winter, slugs are less active, just be sure to remove any you notice. We often find one or two while picking salad, and either squash or cut them or throw them to the hens. Less frequent watering helps reduce their presence, as does the absence of weeds and an occasional, careful look under any larger leaves.

Picking salad leaves

Good harvesting is as important as good growing, so here is a brief summary of advice to help you obtain the greatest number of healthy indoor leaves over a long period.

- Make sure that plants have enough space – say, 20x20cm (8x8"); half that in containers.
- Pick rather than cut, gently twisting leaves with a slight downward push.
- Pick all larger, outer leaves – probably fortnightly or longer in midwinter, then weekly in March and April.
- Plants survive frost better when small, but not too small: check the photos for size comparisons in different seasons.
- Remove and compost any yellow, holed or other leaves you don't want to eat: this keeps plants in good health and reduces slug presence.

All salad plants, including lettuce, endive, chicory, Chinese cabbage, rocket, pak choi, spinach, sorrel and mizuna, can be cropped in this way. See the next chapter for winter salads, and some other vegetables, that you can grow indoors.

Chapter 15

An amazing array of vegetables

Salads, roots and leaves to grow indoors in winter

The vegetables described in this chapter can all be grown in cool soil with low levels of light, and they tolerate being frozen as well. They include salads of many kinds, as well as beetroot, carrots, chard, radishes, spinach, sorrel and turnips. In all cases I emphasise the importance of sowing in good time before winter, but not too early, so that plants are at their fittest and strongest before being virtually 'closed down' in midwinter.

The three periods of winter growth

It helps to have a clear idea of how growth patterns alter markedly between autumn and spring.

Late autumn, roughly late October to mid-December, is characterised by rapidly decreasing temperature and daylight. Even mild days in November see little growth at British latitudes, because light is so pale and brief. Yet six weeks before that, plants are still growing fast, hence the need to sow many of these seeds by mid-September.

Midwinter is an empty period of small, precious growth, from about mid-December to mid-February. Any new leaves are small and thin.

Late winter / early spring, from mid-February to April, brings a dramatic and quite sudden change to growing again strongly, as light levels and temperature increase, starting around Valentine's Day under cover. Mild spells in March can stimulate quite a lot of new growth in just a few days, on plants that have been establishing root systems since October.

Right: Leaf radish flowering in April. The flowers are full of radish flavour.

Three seasons in a tunnel
1. Recently planted salads in October, underneath some mostly de-leafed tomatoes, which continued for another fortnight.
2. The same tunnel from the other end in February, when some snow has blown in the open door over plants of wild rocket.
3. The same view in April, with the wild rocket just visible in foreground: all outer leaves have been picked about 15 times, and mustards, pak choi and rocket are starting to flower.

Timings of sowings

From the dates just described, there are *four months* – October to January – when sowing is barely viable for having crops to harvest in winter under cover. Therefore, make a note to sow seed in September, by mid-month for most vegetables (see table, page 204), enabling the autumn period to be used by seedlings to develop into robust plants before winter.

Sowing for fleece & cloches

Overwintering salads and vegetables to be grown under fleece or a cloche should be sown and planted a fortnight earlier than the timings given in this chapter, which are for polytunnels, greenhouses and conservatories. Sow mostly in late August and early September, plant in September's second and third weeks, then lay fleece or cover with a cloche by the end of October.

Sowing in modules

Raising plants in their own mini 'pot' of compost, for planting out after three or four weeks, is a great way of starting a wonderful range of seedlings at the same time as allowing summer vegetables to finish growing. Some plastic module trays have 60 cells and are little more than A4 size.

One tray of 60 cells can be sown with seeds of many different vegetables, which can then all be planted at the same time to create a bed with many different harvests.

Tray in mid-October, ready to plant, from mid-September sowing. From left: mustard 'Green in the Snow', pak choi 'Red Lady', pak choi 'Bonzai', mizuna 'Red Knight', chicory 'Castel-franco', land cress, mustard 'Red Frills', lettuce 'Grenoble Red', salad rocket, winter purslane.

Seedlings that grow at the same rate

Seeds from any of these three groups can be sown at the same time and planted out together. The time in weeks is from sowing to having plants ready to go in the ground, when sown under cover in autumn.

Extra fast (under three weeks): leaf radish, mizuna.
Fast (three or four weeks): most oriental leaves – Chinese cabbage, komatsuna, mibuna, mustards, pak choi and tatsoi, also kale and rockets.
Medium (four or five weeks): spinach, chard, lettuce, endive, chicory, winter purslane.
Slowest (five to seven weeks): corn salad (lamb's lettuce), land cress, sorrel, parsley, coriander, chervil.

An easy way of grouping seed is, for example, to buy a pack of mixed oriental salad seeds.

The seeds of all the plants covered here can be stored for two years, so I recommend buying a mixture of named varieties. You can then grow more of what you like. Mustard 'Red Frills', for instance, is a favourite with many people.

A–Z of vegetables for growing under cover

The sowing dates given in the following text and summarised in the table overleaf are for walk-in structures such as polytunnels, greenhouses and conservatories; they can be brought forward a fortnight for growing under cloches and fleece over winter. This precision is to give you the best date, but a week on either side is usually possible.

Spacings are mostly for planting out and are nearly all the same, 20-25cm (8-10") apart in all directions. Row spacings are given for seeds that grow well from direct sowing, usually 25-30cm (10-12") rows with 10-20cm (4-8") between plants, except for closer-spaced carrots and salad onions.

Indoor vegetables for winter					
Vegetable	Sow*	Plant	Space (cm)**	Harvest	Comments
Beetroot	Early Sept	Oct	20-30	Feb–May	Leaves mostly
Carrot	Early Oct	n/a	1x20-30	Apr–May	Slugs in Oct
Chard / leaf beet	Aug–mid-Sept	Sept–early Oct	20-30	Oct–May	Salad and cooking
Chervil	Early Sept	Oct	20-25	Oct–April	Productive
Chicory (leaf)	Early Sept	Oct	20	Nov–May	Try 'Castelfranco'
Chinese cabbage	Mid-Sept	Early Oct	20-25	Nov–Apr	Slugs
Coriander	Late Aug–Sept	Sept–Oct	20-30	Nov–May	Productive
Corn salad	Late Sept	n/a	10x20	Jan–Apr	Mildew possible
Endive	Early–mid-Sept	Oct	20-30	Nov–May	For leaves or hearts
Kale	Late Aug–Sept	Sept–Oct	20-40	Nov–May	Salad and cooking
Komatsuna	Mid-Sept	Oct	20-25	Nov–Apr	Fast but slugs
Land cress	Sept	Oct	20	Nov–May	Extra hardy
Lettuce (heart)	Mid-Sept	Mid–late Oct	22-25	Apr–early May	Aphid risk
Lettuce (leaf)	Early–mid-Sept	Oct	22	Nov–June	Certain varieties
Mizuna	Late Sept–Oct & Jan–early Feb	Oct–Nov & Feb	20-25	Nov–May	Productive
Mustards	Mid-Sept	Oct	20-25	Nov–Apr	Huge variety
Onion, salad	Late Aug–Sept	Late Sept–Oct	20-25	Mar–May	Easy to grow
Pak choi	Early–mid-Sept	Sept–mid-Oct	20-25	Nov–Apr	Slugs
Parsley	July–early Aug	Sept	20-25	Oct–May	Slow to establish
Peas for shoots	Jan–Feb	Feb–Mar	20	Apr–June	Top flavour
Radish (leaf)	Mid–late Sept, Jan–early Feb	Oct & Feb	20	Nov–Apr	Some disease
Radish (root)	Feb–Apr	n/a	1x20	Apr–May	Rapid
Rocket, salad	Mid–late Sept	Oct	20-25	Nov–May	Varietal differences
Rocket, wild	Late Aug–Sept	Sept–Oct	25-30	Nov–Dec & Mar–June	Quiet in winter
Sorrel, broad-leaved	Early Sept	Oct	25	Nov–May	Productive
Sorrel, buckler-leaved	Mar–Aug	May–Oct	30	Mar–Nov	Small salad leaves
Spinach	Early–mid-Sept	Early Oct	20-25	Nov–May	Salad and cooking
Tatsoi	Mid-Sept	Early Oct	20	Nov–early Apr	Early to flower
Turnip	Feb–Mar	n/a	7x25-30	Apr–May	Leaves and roots
Winter purslane	Sept	Oct	25-30	Nov–Apr	Delicious flowers

* Sow two weeks earlier for growing under fleece and cloches.

** Spacings in the table are mostly for planting out: see text for spacings when sowing direct. (NB 2.5cm = 1")

Clumps of overwintered 'Red Frills' mustard in a polytunnel in April, now about to flower.

Beetroot

Growth of beetroot is extremely slow in winter, and the leaves turn a darker red than usual. Patience is rewarded with salad leaves from March and small roots from April.

Varieties

'Bulls Blood' for dark red leaves, 'Boltardy' for an attempt at early roots.

Sowing & planting

Sow in the first half of September, no later. Sowing in pots or modules works well: sow three seeds in each, and thin to four plants.

Spacing

Allow 20cm (8") for salad leaves, 30cm (12") for roots.

Harvests

It's best not to harvest salad leaves before February, to allow roots to grow. Then keep picking small leaves until bolting in May, or if left unpicked there should be small roots by April.

Problems

Nothing too bad – slugs may nibble roots and leaves a little.

Carrot

Pull any weeds while small, to keep the soil bare between plants, helping to minimise slug numbers. The main difficulty with carrots is establishing the seedlings before winter.

Varieties

'Early Nantes' makes fair-sized, stump-rooted carrots; the roots of 'Amsterdam Forcing' are thinner and a little quicker to develop.

Sowing

Sowing in the first week of October allows small plants to establish before winter and stay small enough to resist the cold. Earlier sowings can result in less hardy plants, with a risk of bolting in the spring. If you miss this time, sowing in late February to early March is good for carrots in May.

Sow in very clean soil with no weeds nearby. Water the soil thoroughly before sowing, and not afterwards, for about six weeks, to keep the surface dry and discourage slugs.

Spacing

Sow in rows 20-30cm (8-12") apart and thin carrots to about 1cm (½") apart.

Harvests

From about March there may be thinnings to enjoy, and by April some larger roots can be pulled or eased out with a trowel. Harvest roots here and there to allow room for remaining ones to grow large.

Problems

Establishing seedlings can be difficult because of slugs; after that, there are no carrot root flies at this time of year so roots should be healthy.

Chard / leaf beet

The dormant period for chard is longer than for many salads, then growth is fast from about the middle of March until flowering in May.

Varieties

'Rainbow chard' gives a nice range of coloured stems; any leaf beet is good.

Sowing & planting

Sow from August to the middle of September. Slugs like chard and leaf beet, so after watering seedlings or young plants in well, leave dry for a fortnight until established.

Spacing

Allow 20cm (8") for salad leaves, 30cm (12") for large chard and beet leaves.

Harvests

Push stems down as you twist them off, or cut them, to avoid uprooting plants: harvest larger leaves from the outside and don't cut across the top of plants, which results in cutting the small growing tips, leading to slower re-growth.

Problems

None, apart from slugs.

Chervil

Chervil likes moist soil and is not too bothered by any pests in winter. In cool soil and with little light, it grows faster than parsley.

Varieties

'Brussels Winter' is a little hardier than common chervil, although both prefer winter cold to summer heat.

Sowing & planting

Sow any time in September; early in the month if you want several pickings before winter. Sowing three or four seeds in a module works well, for planting a clump of anything from one to three plants. Or sow one 1.2m (4') row for plenty to harvest, with plants thinned to 10cm (4") apart.

Spacing

Allow 20-25cm (8-10") between plants.

Harvests

Outer stems can be cut or picked individually. Keep some medium-sized leaves on plants through winter and they will then re-grow

Picking leaves of chervil in November: twisting stems gently to remove their whole length where possible, keeping plants tidy for the next harvest.

more quickly in late February. Then leaves are abundant until flowering begins after the middle of April.

Problems
None.

Chicory (leaves)
Chicory is easy to grow, but learning to like the leaves' bitterness is perhaps more difficult. They are diluted by mixing with other strong-flavoured leaves such as chervil, sorrel and mustards.

Varieties
For an abundance of green leaves speckled with red, try 'Castelfranco', and for dark red leaves grow 'Treviso' and 'Palla Rossa' types. Even if described as hearting chicories they can be picked for outer leaves. They are more robust than lettuce, with fewer fungal problems.

Sowing & planting
Sow preferably in the first half of September. Two or three seeds in modules can be thinned to one seedling after a fortnight.

Spacing
A spacing of 20cm (8") is good.

Harvesting 'Castelfranco' chicory in early March in the polytunnel.

Harvests
Midwinter pickings of outer leaves are tricky as they lie close to the soil, but they usually snap off, stem and all, when twisted. Then by March it becomes easier and leaves are abundant until flowering in May.

Problems
Slugs like newly planted chicory and the stems of its older leaves, which can be pinched off after picking, but there is no susceptibility to mildew.

Chinese cabbage
This fast-growing plant, which thrives in cool conditions, is ideal for leaves in winter if your soil is sandy and slug free; otherwise beware the molluscs' liking for it. Growing for a heart in March or April is also possible.

Varieties
Any variety should work; the availability changes every year. A new red one called 'CN 1604 F1' (see photos, pages 119-120), bred for leaves rather than heart, shows promise and has survived winter under a fleece outdoors. There are many green varieties for hearting.

Sowing & planting
The middle of September is best for sowing, to have a strong plant for early October. Be sure to sow only in slug-free soil, or to set out strong, healthy plants, from modules with one plant in each, which should then survive any early nibbles.

Spacing
Allow 20cm (8") for leaves; for a heart, plant at 25cm (12").

Harvests
For leaves, use a knife or gentle downward pressure to pick outer leaves, and be prepared to cut a few slugs too, or compost them with any damaged leaves. Harvests accelerate in late winter before flowering by early April.

Leave plants alone if you hope for a heart, which should develop in late March and April but will not be very dense before a flower stem appears out of it, probably in late April.

Problems

Slugs are usually eating some leaves whatever the season, making this a difficult vegetable to grow well.

Coriander

Coriander is extremely hardy and may survive outdoors without protection, but growing it under cover will give many more harvests over a long period.

Varieties

'Calypso' thrives in cold conditions and grows for longer in spring.

Sowing & planting

Late August to early September is best for sowing; sowings in early August may flower before Christmas. Sow two or three seeds and thin to one plant per module for easier picking. Planting is straightforward, with no pests to worry about.

Spacing

Allow 20-25cm (8-10") for strong, healthy plants with thick stems.

Harvests

Pick larger stems continually and there should be an abundance in November and again in March and April, even into May when flowering stems can be stripped of their tasty leaves and flowers.

Problems

Pinch off any browning leaves.

Corn salad

My experience is of healthier growth outdoors, with less mildew on leaves, but I have seen good plants of lamb's lettuce (corn salad) indoors, sown at the right time and kept moist.

Varieties

Large-leaved varieties, such as 'D'Orlanda' and 'Louviers', give the best pickings.

Sowing

Sowing direct works best: mid- to late September sowings ensure that plants are well

This coriander was sown in late August, planted early October and picked lightly before Christmas. After being frozen many times, some leaves had brown fungal infections and were picked off, but there are now healthy new leaves in late February.

established but not too large before winter. Earlier sowings are at risk of mildew.

Spacing
Space more closely than for other salads: aim for rows of 20cm (8") apart with 10cm (4") between plants.

Harvests
The first and largest central rosette can be cut in January or February, leaving some stem below, which will then throw out a second harvest of smaller rosettes for cutting every two or three weeks until flowering in April.

Problems
Mildew on under-watered or overheated plants is the main difficulty. Sow at the right time and keep the soil moister than for other leaves, especially at first and then again in spring.

Endive (leaves & hearts)
Endives are hardier than lettuce and less prone to fungal infection, so it is worth appreciating their more bitter flavour, or dressing leaves sweetly.

Varieties
Frizzy endives such as 'Plantation' and 'Frenzy' can crop well either side of midwinter. For larger, less serrated leaves try 'Bubikopf'.

Sowing & planting
The first weed of September is best for sowing, and up to mid-month. Sow two or three seeds per module and thin to one. Recently set-out plants are liked by slugs, so a torchlit patrol is worthwhile after planting endives.

Spacing
A spacing of 20cm (8") is generally good, or 30cm (12") for larger leaves and hearts in spring.

Endive 'Plantation' in early March after picking. These plants have produced all winter.

Harvests
For hearting in late March and April, wait until the central leaves are showing some blanched effect with a slight yellowing.

For leaves, picking of outer leaves can begin in late October, and if plants are not picked too hard they can offer many fair-sized leaves throughout winter. There should be an abundance of lovely leaves from March to early May.

Problems
Slugs at planting time, as for chicory. Also there is often slug damage to stems of lower leaves, which can be pinched off after picking.

Kale
Kale for large leaves is best grown outdoors, otherwise it takes a lot of precious space indoors. However, the advice here is for both large leaves to cook with and small leaves to eat in salad.

Varieties
For salad kale, grow the pretty, flat-leaved 'Red Russian' and dark green 'Cavolo Nero'. They can also produce large leaves for cooking.

This 'Red Russian' kale in April, already picked many times for salad leaves, continued until early May.

Sowing & planting

August sowings can grow large by November, if you have allowed space, otherwise sow by about the middle of September.

One to three plants in a clump is possible, depending on whether you want many small leaves or a few larger ones.

Spacing

Give plants 20-40cm (8-16"), according to the size of leaves wanted.

Harvests

Start in November with larger leaves from below, always the bottom-most ones, and remove any yellowing ones at the same time to help plants keep healthy. Always leave around six to eight leaves on each stem so that plants can photosynthesise enough energy to re-grow more quickly. Flowering stems in May are as tasty as sprouting broccoli.

Problems

Watch for slugs at planting time. Some grey aphids may appear later on the undersides of leaves: they can be washed off.

Komatsuna

A rather difficult vegetable to grow but worth trying for its speed of growth and tender leaves of mild flavour, especially when young.

Varieties

This is often offered simply as 'komatsuna' or 'mustard spinach', but some new red varieties are coming through and are worth trying for their greater resistance to slugs, as well as their wonderful colour – although they grow more slowly.

Sowing & planting

Sow in the middle of September, for planting before mid-October. Sow three or four seeds per module to have one or two plants in a clump.

Red komatsuna in the tunnel in early March, close to flowering and its colour sadly faded.

Land cress in a polytunnel in February. Sown in September, it has been just picked of a few leaves.

Four-week-old plants are usually strong enough to resist slugs when planted.

Spacing

A spacing of 20cm (8") is good for salad leaves, or 25cm (10") for larger leaves to stir-fry.

Harvests

Cut or twist off large leaves from November, although they may have some slug holes. Leaves can be bountiful in March; flowering is from March and leaf colour diminishes.

Problems

Slugs: remove any you find, and check by night with a torch just after planting.

Land cress

Land cress leaves have a peppery bite, most invigorating in winter, and plants keep producing through cool weather indoors, suffering few problems with pests or diseases.

Varieties

There is no varietal distinction at present.

Sowing & planting

September is good for sowing: later sowings can work but harvests will then be small until March. Sow three or four seeds per module, thinned to one or two, with plants still quite small but ready for planting after four weeks; or sow direct in rows 25cm (10") apart.

Spacing

Allow 20cm (8") for module plants or 10x20cm (4x8") in rows.

Harvests

Large outer leaves can be picked all through winter when plants are not picked too hard, about the size of those in the photo above or a little smaller. The flowering stems in April and early May are pretty and also have a good taste, although pungent.

Problems

None indoors.

Lettuce (hearts)

Lettuce hearts form in spring on plants sown in September, and survive winter at a small to medium size.

Varieties

'Valdor' and 'Marvel of Four Seasons' are

All these lettuces were sown on 10 September and picked of outer leaves until March, then one was left unpicked. Now, on 3 May, it has a fine heart.

green- and red-tinged butterheads. Cos lettuce such as 'Winter Density' will resist frost but suffer more from slugs, while 'Grenoble Red' makes a crisp heart but needs to be well watered when hearting in April and early May.

Sowing, planting & spacing

Between 10 and 15 September is ideal for sowing. Treat as for leaf lettuce, below, but allowing a little more room between plants, say 22-25cm (9-10").

Harvests

Hearts begin to tighten after about the middle of March, and by April you should see some looking ready. Cut some as soon as hearts are forming, because by early May they will start to split open as they move towards flowering.

Problems

See leaf lettuce, below. Also, aphids are more likely in hearts than on leaf lettuce – water is the best remedy.

Lettuce (leaves)

Picking lettuce for its outer leaves can keep plants productive throughout winter, and even until June.

Varieties

'Grenoble Red' has proved itself time and again in my polytunnels as a leaf lettuce; 'Freckles' also survives well but is a little more attractive to slugs. 'Mottistone' has pretty leaves and 'Cocarde', whose leaves are a little more bitter, is prolific.

Sowing & planting

Early September gives more leaves in autumn; around 15 September is the final sowing date for plants to establish well before winter. Sow two seeds per module, thinned to one, or in a seed tray and prick out into modules, seed trays or small pots.

Plants are ready after about four weeks but can stay in modules for up to six weeks from the sowing date, for planting before the last week in October.

Spacing

A spacing of 22cm (9") allows room for plenty of leaves to develop over a long period.

Outer leaves can be picked off in November and a few in December, so that plants are not too large before being frosted – small leaves are less damaged by frost. January is a lean time, then from February harvests can be fortnightly, and weekly from March, with leaves that are bigger and glossier each time. I find that the same plants of 'Grenoble Red' can be picked weekly until the middle of June, by which time they are nine months old – quite extraordinary really.

Problems

Watch for slugs at planting time and maintain some airflow: any lack of ventilation will result in mildew on older leaves and even a rotting of the stem – lettuce does better in a cool draught than in cosseted warmth.

Mizuna sown late September and unpicked till January: it can be harvested of a few leaves or left to grow.

Mizuna

Mizuna is a most reassuring plant, fast growing and with an abundance of slightly peppery leaves that are not too hot to be a staple in the salad bowl. Its close relative mibuna has longer, thinner leaves and is rather less productive.

Varieties

Many green varieties are good: I like 'Waido' for its chunky stems. I have also had success with various purple- and red-leaved mizunas such as 'Red Knight F1'.

Sowing & planting

Sow late September to early October – later than other salads, because of mizuna's speed of growth. Earlier sowings will peak before Christmas and may not survive the frosts of winter. Mizuna's speed of growth makes a January sowing possible, to plant in February, for leaves in late March and April, and flowers in May.

Sow two seeds thinned to one per module, or in rows 25cm (10") apart. Germination should be rapid.

Spacing

Give plants 20-25cm (8-10") each way or 15cm (6") apart in rows.

Harvests

Although mizuna can be cut when large, up to two or three times, it can also be picked for its larger leaves, giving smaller but regular harvests for up to five months. Even when it starts to flower, regular picking of the tasty stems and flowers should keep it growing for another three weeks or so.

Problems

Plants recover strongly from the nibbles of slugs and woodlice. I have had mizuna plants eaten almost to invisibility in November and December, then survive frost and darkness before re-growing strongly and abundantly from about the middle of February.

Mustard

Mustard is easy to grow and comes in many shapes, flavours and colours; if you are wary of peppery leaves, try the 'Frills' varieties, which have a milder flavour.

Varieties

There are many possibilities, such as 'Green in the Snow' for a high yield of extremely peppery leaves, 'Red Frills' for elegant, deeply serrated and crimson-red leaves (more coloured in cold weather), 'Pizzo' for frilly-edged green leaves, and 'Giant Red' for leaves to stir-fry. 'Green in the Snow' (picked small) and 'Red Frills' are the most productive for salads.

Sowing & planting

The second and third week of September are about right for sowing, for planting by the middle of October.

Multi-sowing of modules works well, to have two or three plants in each, or seedlings can be thinned to one plant per station for easier picking of larger leaves.

Spacing

Allow 20cm (8") for smaller leaves, 25cm (10") for larger ones. Plants will quickly fill the space.

Harvests

From November and until Christmas there should be quite a few leaves, and if plants are not picked too hard you may have some nice pickings in January and February. Then by March there will be an abundance, until early or mid-April, when the first flowering stems result in a slowing of leaf production.

Problems

There are no major difficulties, although slugs and woodlice can cause damage at planting time and enjoy warming themselves with nibbles of the hottest leaves, 'Giant Red' and 'Green in the Snow'.

Extreme frost can lead to rotting of stems, especially with the 'Frills' varieties.

Onion, salad

Small onions look fragile but are hardy to many extremes of weather and suffer few pest or disease problems, especially in winter. Alliums are good in tunnels for crop rotation, and garlic grows well from autumn planting.

Varieties

'White Lisbon Winter Hardy' grows really well indoors, or 'Ishikura' for longer stems.

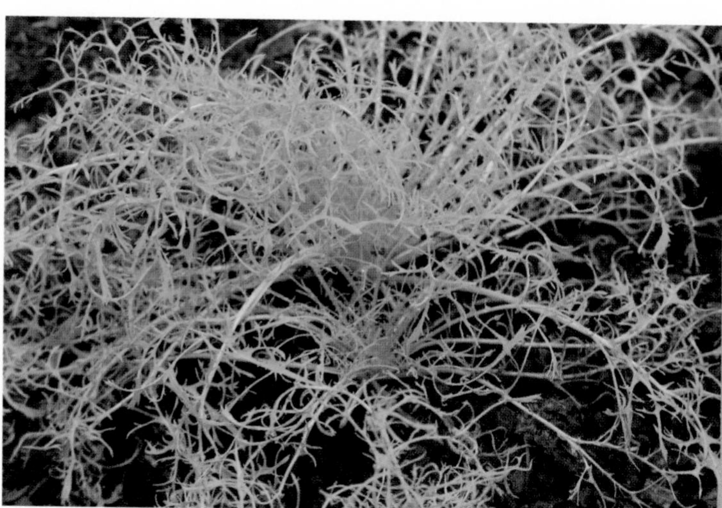

'Green Frills' (also called 'Golden Streaks') mustard, two plants in a clump, in February in the polytunnel. This was sown mid-September and has been picked of some outer leaves and yellowing leaves.

This clump of three pak choi plants, variety 'Joi Choi', in the tunnel in February, was sown in early September and has been harvested of salad leaves, with some slug-eaten leaves removed.

Sowing, planting out & spacing

Sow late August to mid-September. Sow eight or ten seeds in modules or small pots and avoid excess warmth while they are germinating. Plant out whole clumps at 20-25cm (8-10"), in late September or until the middle of October. Earlier plantings may be ready by Christmas but should also survive as quite large plants until needed, and grow strongly from March.

Harvests

Pull whole bunches, or the largest onion of each bunch, when they are the size you like. Careful harvesting of individual onions can make the harvest last for up to three months if you sowed a few in late August and a few in the middle of September.

Problems

None are likely.

Pak choi

Although a tricky vegetable to grow, especially because of its vulnerability to slugs, plants produce some tasty leaves in winter and become highly productive in March and April.

Varieties

'Joi Choi F1' grows dark green leaves on pure white stems and has excellent winter hardiness. 'Red Lady F1' is worth growing for pretty leaves but is less productive.

Sowing & planting out

The second week of September is best for sowing. For salad leaves, sow four seeds per module or pot to have two or three for planting in clumps. For large leaves, sow two seeds and thin to one plant.

Plant out before the middle of October to give them time to establish well before winter.

Spacing

Space at 20-25 cm (8-10"), for smaller or larger leaves.

Harvests

Cut stems of larger leaves with a knife, being careful not to disturb the fragile, shallow roots. Light pickings are possible from November and through to February, then, by spring, when plants are more established, leaves are larger and stems can be gently twisted off. Pinch off (and eat) flowering stems in April to keep plants productive until the month's end. Red pak choi flowers earlier and loses leaf colour.

Problems

Slugs are tricky and leaves are often holed at planting time when they are weak, but I find that most pak choi recover after two or three weeks; caterpillars may also make a lot of holes in autumn leaves. By contrast, pak choi in March and April often enjoys a few weeks of glory and looks the picture of health.

Parsley

Flat-leaved parsley is especially hardy but rises to flower earlier than curly parsley. I recommend sowing a few seeds of each for the variety of leaves and a longer harvest.

Varieties

The choice is between any variety of curled and any of flat-leaved parsley: the latter produces more leaves in winter but flowers earlier in spring.

Sowing & planting

Because parsley germinates and grows so slowly, it is best sown around the middle of July and certainly no later than early August, to allow enough time to establish a productive winter plant.

It works well to sow in a seed tray for pricking out after about three weeks, or you can sow three to four seeds in modules or pots. Parsley can be grown as either a clump of two or three together, or as one plant on its own.

Spacing

Allow good space for roots to develop, 20-25cm (8-10"), or set plants in 20cm (8") pots for an indoor windowsill. One pot, filled with good compost, can be impressively productive for several months.

Harvests

Plants take time to establish: the first pickings may be in October but don't pick too hard before winter. Then from late February you should have plenty of new leaves, until flowering in April for flat-leaved and in May for curly. Picking flower stems will prolong plants' life for up to a month, but leaves become smaller.

Problems

Nothing major, except coping with slow initial growth, and an abundance towards the end. Severe frost may damage stems but plants should re-grow.

Pea shoots

These are more for the hungry gap than for winter. I have tried overwintering pea plants but with little success and find they are often overtaken by January sowings, which have not suffered too much cold and dark.

Varieties

'Tall Sugar Snap' is my favourite, for its healthy vigour and hardiness; if you can't find it, choose any tall variety that is described as growing to 1.5-1.8m (5-6'), such as 'Alderman'.

Sowing & planting

Peas should overwinter, but sowing in January for planting in February is as reliable, and brings them to harvest by April, when other winter-salad plants are starting to flower.

'Tall Sugar Snap' pea plants, sown in January and planted February; by April some shoots are ready.

Sowing in small pots on a windowsill is good, to avoid mice eating the seed outside. Three seeds per pot will make for a nice clump with plenty of shoots. When sowing under cover outdoors, I find it worth keeping a primed mousetrap near to the germinating seeds.

Spacing
A spacing of 20cm (8") is about right; a little wider results in more shoots as plants grow larger in late May.

Harvests
Wait until plants are 20-30cm (8-12") high, then pinch or cut off the top 5cm (2") to eat. After another fortnight or so, new shoots of the same length should be ready to harvest again. Keep picking as they appear – for a time in May they are juicy and numerous, before becoming thinner in June, when harvests become less worthwhile. See Chapter 11, page 166, for details of growing early pea shoots outdoors.

Problems
Mice eating seeds is the main problem – see 'Sowing & planting', left.

Radish (leaves)
A mild taste of radish is welcome in winter salads, and these leaves grow to a good size, but plants are a little more vulnerable to extreme frost than other oriental leaves.

Varieties
'Sai Sai' is good for green leaves; 'Sangria' for red-stemmed leaves is less productive. Some leaf radish has no varietal name.

Sowing & planting
The second half of September works well for sowing, a little later than other salads. Two or three seeds per pot or module should germinate rapidly, then remove any weak seedlings. Plants want to be in the ground by mid-October because they are vulnerable to slugs.

You can also sow seeds in January and February for eating either as seedling baby leaves or as slightly larger leaves, before they flower in late April.

Spacing
Spacings are the same as for most salads, around 20cm (8").

Harvests
Fast growth means some good harvests of outer leaves before Christmas, and again in March and April. If leaves are left unpicked, and there is no severe frost (below about -10°C/14°F), a long white radish root will develop and wants eating before the plants flower in mid-April.

Problems
Leaf radish is prone to fungal infection: remove any brown spotted leaves and the odd plant that rots completely.

Radish (roots)
Radishes grow more healthily in late winter than in midwinter, but their speed of growth means April harvests are possible from February sowings. Red radishes are a welcome sight in early spring.

Leaf radish has large seed, and its cotyledons, pictured here, can be eaten as micro-leaves.

Varieties

Old 'Cherry Belle' varieties grow lovely round, red roots, or try 'French Breakfast' types for longer, white and red roots.

Sowing & planting

Sow from early February, then sow again six weeks later, to have a succession of roots.

Sow direct in drills about 20cm (8") apart, with seeds no more than 1cm (½") apart. Some thinning is often needed because radishes growing too thickly make plenty of leaves but tiny roots.

Harvests

As soon as you see small coloured roots, a few of the largest can be gently pulled out, leaving the others to grow some more. Two months of harvests are possible from two late-winter sowings, as on page 217.

Problems

Slugs may nibble some roots, which may also become hollow and fibrous as they grow large – you just need to eat them more quickly.

Rocket, salad

If you like peppery leaves, salad rocket is a winter 'banker' for its hardiness and an ability to grow at low temperatures. Its flavour is less hot than wild rocket.

Varieties

Plain 'Salad Rocket' is good; also 'Apollo' for larger and rounder leaves, which are less peppery, although older plants have hotter leaves.

Sowing & planting

Sow in the middle of September and into the third week. Earlier sowing is possible but may result in less healthy leaves in late winter. Sow two to four seeds per pot or module, to grow one or two plants per station, and planting is possible until the end of October. Slugs are magnificently uninterested in rocket.

This salad rocket in February has survived winter in good health and is now growing strongly.

Spacing

A spacing of 20-25cm (8-10") for each clump is good; wider for large leaves.

Harvests

The first harvests in November are of a few large leaves, then as plants age they send out more numerous, smaller leaves. By March there will also be flowering stems, which want removing – their buds and small leaves are edible – and plants should continue in semi-flowering mode through April, with plenty of small leaves too. By May it becomes harder to find worthwhile leaves, and wild rocket (see below) takes centre stage, with abundant leaves in May and June.

Problems

Rocket is prone to yellow and brown spots on older leaves, which are best removed to make the healthy leaves easier to pick.

Rocket, wild

Hot, thin leaves of wild rocket are not a salad staple; one or two clumps may provide enough leaves, which are valuable in May and June when the other peppery leaves have finished.

Varieties

This is usually offered as just wild rocket.

Sowing & planting

Sow any time in late August or early September, to have well-established plants before Christmas. Sow three or four seeds per pot or module; plants may be set out when still small.

Spacing

Space a little wider than salad rocket on account of wild rocket's longevity: 25-30cm (10-12") is good.

Harvests

Cutting works well since there are so many small leaves. Be sure to cut *above* the small new leaves, not into main stems. Before winter, if plants are still small, I would pick any larger leaves rather than cutting them all. Plants then go semi-dormant in winter and want cleaning of old, yellow leaves in late February so that from the middle of March new growth can be harvested through spring off clean plants, with leaves all healthy.

Clumps need two or three weeks to re-grow after each cutting, and they eventually flower in June. Wild rocket is perennial and can be left to grow through the summer, for harvesting again in autumn and spring, but a second season's growth is less vigorous. It will also drop a *lot* of seeds if you leave its flowers unpicked.

Problems

Some leaves develop brown and yellow spots in damp winter weather, but usually when picked off there is healthier re-growth as the days lengthen. Flea beetle damage to leaves is less of a problem in winter and under cover than in spring and summer outside.

Sorrel

Two different types give long harvests.

Varieties

Broad-leaved sorrel is the most common type and the best for growing in winter. Buckler-leaved sorrel is delicious in salads but goes mostly dormant from December to early March, before growing through spring and summer.

Broad-leaved sorrel indoors in April. Sown in August, it has been picked of many leaves through winter. Pinching off flower stems in summer kept it producing in the next winter too.

'Medania' spinach in April. The leaf shape has changed to more pointed, a fortnight before flowering.

Sowing & planting

Sow from late August to early September, for clumps to be well established by winter. Tiny seed makes it difficult to sow precisely: aim for three or four seeds per pot or module, thinned to one or two, and plant after four or five weeks.

Buckler-leaved sorrel likes the warmth of indoor spaces and can be kept going as a perennial plant, for leaves from spring to autumn. Sow from March to August and plant from May to October.

Spacing

Sorrel is vigorous when established, so 25-30cm (10-12") is good.

Harvests

Keep picking larger and also older, dark green leaves, as well as removing holed or yellow leaves, which often have a slug attached. By April you may have too many leaves but they can be used in many ways – salads, soups, omelettes and to flavour stews: sorrel's lemon flavour is a refreshing, clean taste after the starch of winter.

In May, broad-leaved sorrel makes flower stems which, if removed several times over, then cede to leaves again through summer. Buckler-leaved sorrel keeps producing lots of small leaves, as well as flowers in late summer.

Problems

Slugs need watching but rarely kill plants: keep removing them after planting and while picking.

Spinach

Spinach offers leaves for a long period in winter and they change flavour and character all the time, from soft and small to thicker and sweeter, then to longer with fine hairs (see picture above) and again to smaller as plants flower in late April and May.

Varieties

I have tried several varieties and find that 'Medania' gives a steady harvest of dark green leaves; 'Fuji F1' offers a slightly quicker harvest of paler green and longer leaves, quicker to flower in spring as well; and 'Bordeaux' grows plenty of medium-sized, red-stemmed leaves over a long period in winter.

Sowing & planting

Sow from early to mid-September, early is better. An average of three seeds per pot or module should give two or three seeds per clump.

Spacing

Allow 20cm (8") for smaller salad leaves, 25cm (10") for larger leaves.

Harvests

Autumn harvests are often holed by slugs and woodlice, but are still edible and delicious. Any damaged and yellowing leaves are best removed when seen, to reduce slug habitat. By March there will be a growing abundance of healthy new leaves, and by the middle of April you may have too many, until flowering occurs around the middle of May.

Problems

Woodlice can do major damage to young spinach seedlings, evident as serrations around leaf edges and sometimes a collapse of plants as their stem is nibbled: when damage occurs in a propagating area, lift pots or trays and squash any woodlice that are running to hide. Woodlice in soil are more difficult to do anything about – I find the best remedy is to plant by the first week of October, from sowing early September, so that plants have more time to grow away from damage.

Tatsoi

This can be a tricky vegetable, adored by slugs and sometimes with small, fiddly leaves, and it is the first plant of oriental leaves to flower at winter's end. But the leaves are glossy, dark green, tender and delicious.

Some varieties of tatsoi hug the soil but 'Yukina Savoy' has more upright leaves, easier to pick.

Varieties

Named varieties are rare: try 'Supi' and 'Yukina Savoy' if available, for their longer stems that are easier to pick.

Sowing & planting

The second week of September is ideal for sowing. Sow two or three seeds per clump, thinned to one for easier harvesting.

Aim to plant before the middle of October, as tatsoi is a favourite of slugs, and grows away from them better before it becomes too cold and dark.

Spacing
A spacing of 20cm (8") is good.

Harvests
Early growth is often of poor quality, with leaves holed by slugs and caterpillars, which need removing when seen. Subsequent growth should be healthier, with some harvests possible in late autumn, then again in February and March before flowering in early April. The picture on the previous page was taken in late February.

Problems
Slugs, as described.

Turnip
Turnips are versatile to grow, with their best growth coming either side of summer, when they flower. So the early sowing advised here is best harvested as small roots in spring, before roots turn woody as flowering time approaches.

Varieties
I suggest 'Milan Purple Top' and 'Atlantic F1', both possessed of pretty roots, rapid growth and tasty leaves.

Sowing and spacing
In this context, turnip is an early spring vegetable for sowing in February and March, indoors. It is best sown direct in 25-30cm (10-12") rows: the tiny seeds often come up too thickly and seedlings should be thinned to 5-10cm (2-4") apart.

Harvests
A few young leaves can be picked for salad, or you can eat the leaves from thinned plants. Small roots will develop in April and can be pulled as needed – around golf-ball size is good. By May, larger roots risk becoming woody.

Problems
There are not many problems, although slugs may be tempted by seedlings in February, so avoid watering after sowing, for a month or so.

Winter purslane
This is one of the prettiest salads and easy to grow, also good enough at self-seeding to become a weed. Its soft, tender leaves of mild flavour provide a welcome balance to winter's stronger-flavoured leaves. Purslane survives outside but leaves of better quality grow indoors or under fleece.

Varieties
There are no named varieties at present: *Claytonia* is just the Latin name and 'miner's lettuce' is a colloquial, Cornish name, from tin

miners who ate winter purslane with their pasties. In North America the same name is used, from Californian miners who ate it in the 1849 gold rush.

Sowing & planting

Throughout September is possible for sowing: earlier sowings give more leaves in autumn, and later sowings that are picked only lightly before midwinter give bigger harvests in spring, even in January.

The tiny seed cannot be sown precisely. Aim for three or four plants in each clump, after some thinning. If woodlice are suspected, sow in early September so that plants are set out in early October and have time to grow away from being nibbled.

Winter purslane in mid-April, from a September sowing and picked many times already. The pretty flowering leaves and stems are all tender and tasty.

Spacing

25cm (10") allows the vigorous roots to spread a little; planting at 30cm (12") can delay flowering in April.

Harvests

Plants grow as round clumps with long stems and are ready to cut when nearly touching, on the spacings given, any time from November. Leaves are best cut with the knife more vertical than horizontal, trimming the stems of drooping leaves around all sides of each clump and leaving some central leaves to encourage rapid re-growth. A few brown leaves need tidying up each time. By early March there will be some pretty white flowers appearing, first on stems and then on the leaves themselves; the flowers are edible and delicious. Keep harvesting until the end of April, when flower stems become tough. Be gentle when cutting, because these plants have brittle roots and their main stalk risks snapping off at ground level.

Problems

Some leaves turn a dull browny green in frosty weather but are still good to eat. During flowering in spring there are always a few seeds that set and then germinate as a thicket of seedlings the following autumn: I advise removing plants to compost by early May at the latest.

Resources

Suppliers

B&Q, for module trays: see www.diy.com

CN Seeds, Pymoor, Ely, Cambs CB6 2ED, 01353 699413, www.cnseeds.co.uk
An extremely wide range of good seeds in larger quantities.

Ferryman Polytunnels, Bridge Road, Lapford, Crediton, Devon EX17 6AE, 01363 83444, www.ferryman-polytunnels.co.uk
Solid, good-value structures.

The Garlic Farm, Mersley Lane, Newchurch, Isle of Wight PO36 0NR, 01983 865378, www.thegarlicfarm.co.uk
A great range of seed garlic.

Implementations, PO Box 2568, Nuneaton CV10 9YR, 0845 330 3148, www.implementations.co.uk
Copper tools to last, of extremely high quality.

LBS Horticulture, Standroyd Mill, Cottontree, Colne, Lancs BB8 7BW, 01282 873333, www.lbsbuyersguide.co.uk
Large rolls of mesh, netting, plastic, polytunnels and many other accessories.

Organic Plants, Delfland Nurseries Ltd, Benwick Road, Doddington, March, Cambs PE15 0TU, 01354 740553, www.organicplants.co.uk
An excellent selection.

PoshCloche Garden Cloches, Oakfield Lodge, School Lane, Lymington SO41 5QE 01590 671380, www.poshcloche.co.uk
Expensive, long lasting and easy to use.

The Real Seed Catalogue, PO Box 18, Newport, near Fishguard, Pembs SA65 0AA, 01239 821107, www.realseeds.co.uk
A broad selection of good, home-grown seeds and advice on seed saving.

Seeds of Italy, A1 Phoenix Ind. Estate, Rosslyn Crescent, Harrow HA1 2SP, 020 8427 5020, www.seedsofitaly.com
These Franchi seeds are best for endives and chicories.

SEER Centre, Ceanghline, Straloch Farm, Enochdhu, Blairgowrie PH10 7PJ, 01250 881789, www.seercentre.org.uk
Information on minerals and rockdust.

Stormy Hall Seeds, Danby Head, Danby, Whitby, N. Yorks YO21 2NN, 01287 661368, www.stormy-hall-seeds.co.uk
Biodynamic seeds of good pedigree.

Left: Ruby chard under early snow, which it survived. Some roots were dug to grow leaves indoors.

West Riding Organics, Halifax Road, Littleborough, Lancs OL15 0LF, 01706 379944, www.organiccompost.org.uk
I enjoy excellent results from their module compost, which is based on peat sieved out of reservoirs.

Organisations

Biodynamic Agriculture Association (BDAA), Painswick Inn Project, Gloucester Street, Stroud GL5 1QG, 01453 759501, www.biodynamic.org.uk
Biodynamic advice, books, preparations and courses.

Garden Organic (HDRA), Ryton Gardens, Coventry CV8 3LG, 024 7630 3517, www.gardenorganic.co.uk
Information, advice and events.
See also The Organic Gardening Catalogue, 01932 253666, www.organiccatalog.com, for their extensive range of seeds and accessories.

The Good Gardeners Association, 4 Lisle Place, Wotton-Under-Edge, Glous GL12 7AZ, 01453 520322, www.goodgardeners.org.uk
Promotes no-dig gardening.

Organic Growers Alliance, Bradshaw Lane Nursery, Pilling, Preston PR3 6AX, www.organicgrowersalliance.co.uk
A dynamic association of growers who are always swapping ideas and advice.

Royal Horticultural Society (RHS), 80 Vincent Square, London SW1P 2PE, 0845 260 5000, www.rhs.org.uk
Help with all aspects of gardening.

Soil Association, South Plaza, Marlborough Street, Bristol BS1 3NX, 0117 314 5000, www.soilassociation.org.uk
Advice, information, books and inspiration on all matters organic.

Publications and advice

The Biodynamic Sowing and Planting Calendar, Maria Thun. Published annually by BDAA (see 'Organisations'), selling 100,000 copies worldwide each year.

How to Grow Food in Your Polytunnel, Mark Gatter & Andy McKee (2010, Green Books). How to make the most of your polytunnel, all year round.

Organic Gardening: the Natural, No-dig Way, Charles Dowding (2nd edn 2010, Green Books). For advice on summer vegetables too.

The Polytunnel Handbook, Andy McKee & Mark Gatter (2008, Green Books). For advice on choosing and erecting the structure.

Salad Leaves for all Seasons, Charles Dowding (2008, Green Books). A guide to the vast range of salad plants and the best ways of growing them, to enjoy leaves all year.

Successful Gardening Without Digging, James Gunston (1960, The Garden Book Club). A glimpse of gardening in different times, with many tips on inter-sowing and inter-planting, to make the most use of space.

The Winter Harvest Handbook, Eliot Coleman (2009, Chelsea Green). Offers fascinating ideas for growing through deep cold in a bright, continental climate.

www.charlesdowding.co.uk My website has regular updates on seasonal gardening and a wide range of other information, including day courses at Lower Farm.

Index

Page numbers in *italics* refer to illustrations